THE RISK INVOLVED

BY JEFFREY UTZINGER

©2024 by Jeffrey Utzinger
Cover ©2024 by Drew Holden
Interior Design ©2024 by Sydney Bozeman

-First Edition

All rights reserved. No part of this publication may be reproduced or transmitted in any form or by any means, electronic or mechanical, including photocopy, recording, or any information storage or retrieval system, without permission in writing from the publisher.

All names used with permission or given pseudonyms.

Publisher's Cataloguing-in-Publication Data

Utzinger, Jeffrey
The risk involved / written by Jeffrey Utzinger
ISBN: 978-1-953932-30-3

1. Biography & Autobiography: Memoirs I. Title II. Author

Library of Congress Control Number: 2024945902

For Christa, without whom there are no stories

TABLE OF CONTENTS

The Seduction of Place...9

Chemical Reactions..15

Beginner's Luck..23

The Risk Involved...37

Insatiable..59

Filament..65

Swarm Season..75

Forty Days of This..93

Woods Walking..101

You're Going to Hell for This..115

Indefinite Light...133

Walk Away Slowly (You Know You'll Be Back)..................139

White Picket Fences...159

Count Your Chickens...175

Duck..193

Why Don't You Do It Yourself..211

Acknowledgements..229

Additional Acknowledgements..233

About the Author...235

THE SEDUCTION OF PLACE

Girls in sheer dresses with gossamer smiles flutter around my porch light all hours of the night. It's springtime when bees swarm, forty-thousand strong. Crowded bodies dissipate from winter-long hives. Girls with insect-thin arms move with migratory grace, holding drinks, heads tilted back, rocking on heels or dancing. A pleasure to watch pass by my window. Bees, when they swarm, will hang beneath eaves, in hollow trees, a mailbox. Workers cluster around the queen like flesh on a seed. One might think, from a distance, a rain cloud had fallen and gathered on his porch.

I've grown tired of these "hive-like conglomerations of cellular living." One hundred people a day move to this town. Names of apartments: "Willowbrook," "Three Oaks," "Bridge-Hollow Point." Reminders of things buried or razed. My wife has gone out in search of more space. Bees, when they swarm, relocate within days. Drunk with honey when they leave, they are docile in clusters. Aggressive only in protecting a hive. The girls' footsteps above us reverberate the message: *we are living a life of our own.*

They are beautiful to watch, and the boys they attract, engorged on fermented hops and the promise of sex. Tattooed bodies in ritual dance.

THE RISK INVOLVED

Their music rattles my windows. A virgin queen after killing all others lures numerous drones on her maiden flight. She collects over five million sperm. A memory—my wife in a parking lot before we were married. She's spinning in circles, telling me she just broke a date. Shoulder-length hair fans above the tail of her coat. Quarter moon darkness. We can't find my car, just started dating, going to eat, and she's spinning mad. I recall thinking she looked like someone in love.

We can't afford a house, so live in rented rooms. No hammers or busted nails, dirty hands from sheetrock. The risk involved in this economy of energy: ejection hangs over our heads. Bees have no sentimental attachments to home. Capture the queen, the rest will follow. The beautiful girls have been replaced by a quiet family of five. I watched from the window (the drones disappeared) as their delicate arms struggled with a couch. I didn't help, not wanting to see them sans masks in full daylight.

Every night for two weeks I've driven forty miles east to paint the interior walls of more rented rooms. The nesting has begun. Darkness means something in the country. Forty-watt bulbs from overhead lights give off a glow, yellow and dull. I brought a halogen lamp. Paint with the windows closed. The lack of outside artificial light to draw the soft skin girls with waxed legs. I am afraid.

A drone's sole purpose is to mate the queen. His moment of glory. Weeks of lounging with guard bees, eating what the workers bring, cease with the arrival of brood. Patterns along the comb. Driven from the hive, they're left to starve. My wife lived on the second floor and would draw back curtains whenever I'd throw rocks. Whiskey to hold me up. I wonder now, if she'd choose me again, from all the boys moving on the sidewalk beneath her.

I want to build a house of rock and wood. No electricity. No phone. I want a fax machine, though. Send and receive on curled pages. Everything in black and white. I also don't want a divorce. I want a sense of community without neighbors. Without church. I want beautiful girls again but only from a distance. I also don't want to be eighteen. From college to this rent house, I had eleven rooms. That's too much shit to move.

My wife can't sleep without a ceiling fan. The walls are painted, and the furniture and dishes in place. The only fan is in the living room, so we pull out the couch each night. Sleep with metal bars in our backs. I begin a new job in the fall. We live in a new house. Bees don't fly in a straight line. They move in a horizontal jerking motion to see. My cat chases mosquitoes around the walls. He won't touch spiders. I lie awake and listen. I'm living away from people for the first time since I was nine years old. The house is surrounded by trees. I realize my father is not in the next room. That I am responsible for protecting this house I don't own.

I bought a thermometer and watch mercury creep toward the century mark. There's no grass in the quarter-acre yard. An insignificant bit of dirt not to own. It needs a garden. Hope or heat stroke made me buy a rain gauge. I crave grass, so splash dishwater each night in a new spot guided by imaginary grids. Fire ant mounds break the landscape. I boil water in a cracked coffee pot, glass microwavable bowls, quart pans on the stove to scald ants. A shame, really. I want wildlife but should settle for insects.

Wax moths, mice, fire ants, and mites will reside with bees. A hive is a hive. I lived with a friend, two dope dealers, and a girl one summer. A boa constrictor in the bathtub. One-bedroom apartment. After a month and a half, I moved in with my girlfriend. A rule for relationships: one room per person. Wood spiders sprawl in our bathtub each morning. Run along baseboards, in cabinets, behind doors. I need to pick one up and hold it thirty seconds. The thought shakes my shoulders.

Cedars explode—a million seeds drift through my window, threaten to impregnate me. Unpacked boxes, a reminder of this disease of ownership. The need for possessions. Books from garage sales, tools with no garage, cassette tapes with no player. The paperwork is astounding. The girls with gelatin lips and breasts and perfect teeth are gone. I can see them from a distance, promise rings on fingers. Prized possessions given to boys as prodigious as cedars.

The distance between yourself and the page, screen, or pane of glass is not far. It's also not love. The drone dies immediately after mating. The praying mantis. Black widow's bite. Violent love. Beauty in a relationship is directly related to the sensation of having one's guts ripped through one's throat. You've got to swallow the hook.

Treetops have reached the bottom of the sun. I've chosen this time, mid-morning, mid-July to begin a garden, taken my cue from what lives here, so I'll begin small: carrots, onions, and radishes. No aspiring plants. Vegetables only came from gardens when I was young, but that's twenty years in my past. I begin with seed packets. Manufacturer's suggestions. The land does not speak to me, so I approach analytically, contrary to my nature. Two rows of carrots, one of radish, one of green onion, rows twenty feet long, a foot between each. A twenty-foot by twelve-foot plot. It looks good on paper. Most things do.

Mesquite branches from nearby trees serve as markers. Now would be a good time to quit. The promise is always sweeter. The swell that begins in the groin, folds the stomach inward, and increases heart rate makes the afterglow as stale as cigarette smoke. The promise of turned earth brought me here, so I crank the rotor-tiller I borrowed from my parents. Gas and filter, three years old, but I've used a tape measure to mark the land. I'm not about to do maintenance. Blue smoke emerges with the third pull. The blades grab the first tuft of crab grass.

I'm pulled forward, into a desire to live more simply. Or perhaps not at all. Not as I envisioned when I first left home. The plan was to do better than my father. My grandfather. Not move backward. Not farm. Not make a living with back and hands. The kingdom I passed through from the first jilt of the blades to the first rock lasted a second. It passed before I could really enjoy the notion of peasant husbandry. Each time the tiller dips below the surface, it lurches. Rock after rock. The machine bounces across the ground. Top soil is nonexistent. Arms numb before

I make the first pass. My hands should be lashed to the handles for a cowboy grip. Eight seconds is an eternity.

Bees caught from a swarm if hived too early in the day will leave to collect pollen, perhaps never to return. One does not own wild things. One either takes pleasure in them or is beaten down. Wild things are beautiful if nothing else. Anything capable of taking one's breath away is beautiful, no matter how terrifying the experience. Cameramen wander around tornado or hurricane ruins, filming stunned reporters, who feign shock and sadness, but watch their eyes—they're overwhelmed with the sheer beauty of a violent creation.

There are train tracks a few miles from here. The train runs beneath the highway that I take to the city—day in, day out. It runs beside the Colorado River and I can hear its whistle at night when the windows are open. My thoughts are clipped like the rhythm of the wheels carrying men with fedoras and incredibly thin women. They're waving at me from a black and white film, threatening to disappear at the next turn. If I could align my thoughts, my fingers on this keyboard to the clack, to the motion of their hands, perhaps I could follow back through time. Perhaps I could find my way home.

CHEMICAL REACTIONS

Instant coffee is the pepper spray of coffees, an effective weapon to ward off evil—alarm clock's buzz before nine, residue of Shiner Bock, manual labor in a Texas July—it's a poison cloud that never quite dissolves, sticks to the spoon's neck, around the cup's edge, between your teeth, but it's got chemicals, and I'm late for work. Microwave screeches, my hand's halfway in to catch the last bit of radiation, grab the mug of boiling water, the glass jar of grinds, and go. The coffee scum's still spinning as I make a U-turn to beat oncoming traffic, gun it hard to run the red light, and the liquid between my legs, not yet tasted, leaps up to scorch my crotch, and that works too—I'm awake.

I've been awake fourteen minutes, alive for twenty-six years, and it doesn't take eating grinds straight from a jar as I weave down the interstate to make me realize my life is headed a direction I don't want to go. I live for five o'clock, the lunch break, the weekend. I live in a rented room, the eleventh in eight years. I live in a fantasy world because I believe I can escape, and I try, with chemicals.

The sun has peaked, blinds me through the dirty windshield. I punch the turn signal to wash away the grime. Wipers scrape across the glass, but the blue liquid doesn't come. Orange oil light flashes. I'd ignore

THE RISK INVOLVED

the warning, but I've also noticed I have no gas. Horns blare, but fuck 'em—all three lanes, I've made the exit and roll into the Texaco to pour regular unleaded fossil fuel and blue toxic cleaner into my truck. 'Cause we all need more chemicals.

Gas station coffee is half a spoon above instant, but it's got a great hook—chemicals in a Styrofoam cup. I pop the plastic top, set it on the hood to mingle with the fumes, take a pinch of snuff, and pump gas. The constricted blood cells really begin to move—who says I don't exercise? Slow oxygen to the brain, quicken the pulse. Suffocation with the sunrise. One, two. One, two. Breathe shallow. Repeat. Another gulp of coffee. Burn the tongue. Spit. The chemically-dependent runner's high.

Industrial strength chemicals with names I can't pronounce—bromides, oxides, hydrates—greet me as I swing through the chain-link fence. They hit you like forgotten fish. Seep into your car's upholstery, stick to your clothes, your hair, your skin. Follow you home at day's end. Some days a shower doesn't help. You arrive next day, prepped and ready to go. Welcome to Plant Kimacows.

We wear uniforms with pockets, our names stitched to the front. Long sleeves to ward off insect bites, acid burns, the sun, but these things find you when they want you. We wear leather boots, steel-toed, with Chemcoat soles that show quarter-size holes in six months or less—cheap-o deluxe or top of the line. Rubber boots wear out in nine. We wear hard hats—blue, yellow, or white—safety glasses with dark or clear lenses, goggles with elastic straps, and face shields that snap to the sides of the hat. We wear rubber gloves that fill with sweat and leather ones rolled in back pockets. Plastic aprons that stick to your chest. Nylon pants, arm sleeves, and jackets. We wear dust masks and respirators, full-body bunny suits. Self-Contained Breathing Apparatus. We carry tape measures and box cutters, screwdrivers and flashlights, notepads and Magic Markers, ink pens and Ph. Strips. We watch films strips every Thursday with crushed skulls and blistered eyeballs to remind us—this could be you.

We process raw material, sling and stew, mix like mad hatters, package and sell to the big boys in Houston, Pennsylvania, Japan.

Everything from cocaine-like crystals that clean computer chips to fifty-gallon drums that weigh five hundred pounds full of bread preservatives. We even make rocket fuel. Chemicals for the masses.

I am not a chemist, have no background in chemistry, can't check the Ph. of an acid rain puddle, titrate a Bleach sample, calculate an equation, read an HMIS label, but I can cut the tops out of metal drums with an oversized can opener, crush the shells with a forklift, use barrels of sand on a pallet for weight, slice the liners into four pieces, and chunk into a dumpster. I can sand, scrape, and paint every hand rail and platform that corrodes like clockwork every six months with OSHA-approved safety yellow. Paint warning lines around fire extinguishers mounted every fifteen feet with lead-based traffic yellow. Paint tanks the size of white elephants on a ladder, safety harness snug around my waist. Spray paint anything, anybody, tied down or not. Hammer nails to build braces in the beds of eighteen-wheelers to keep hazardous waste in place on the highway and ship liners, even in roller-overs or storms at sea.

I trim branches with chainsaws, smear limb sealant, cut grass, weed eat and edge, water flower beds, wash windows, kill wasps and poison ivy, lay pave stone, weed killer, dig fence posts, clean fence rows, crush stumps, pulverize ants, spread fertilizer. I can use household chemicals.

At ten and two it's smoke 'em if ya got 'em time. Cigarette butts pile up beside the picnic table outside the front gate. Pools of tobacco juice. We dehydrate ourselves with caffeine, coffee if it's below seventy, soft drinks if it's above. Coke eats acid off battery terminals. It's gotta cure cancer. Nicotine addiction is supposedly a sign of chemical imbalance, and judging from the guys I work with, I'd say that's true. They're from all over—Holland, Zaire, Mexico, Japan, North Austin, South Austin, the East side, Uvalde, Temple, Bastrop, and Buda. One big, happy family brought together for a common cause—chemical dependency.

THE RISK INVOLVED

There are guys who went to Vietnam, or spent their youth as migrant workers, grew up with seventeen brothers and sisters. Hitchhiked across Europe. Seen the jails of Juarez. Guys who dropped out of high school, have three Associate's Degrees, speak English as a third language, and not very well. Guys with two ex-wives, cheating on their third, who gamble and drink away half of each paycheck, try to screw Uncle Sam each spring. Guys who have failed a drug test three times. There are family men and deacons, boy scout leaders, and little league coaches. A few you may have a beer with after work. Everyone here has told someone to go to hell at least once, some at least once a day, some only behind other's backs, under their breath. Guys have taken a swing, jabbed with a box cutter, brought a gun to work. There are a few who quit or get fired every six months, but who always come back for the chemicals.

A guy I went to college with got me this job five summers ago. Two years later he drove to a nearby park, walked into the creek, stuck a gun in his mouth, and blew a hole through the back of his head. He was manic-depressive. An alcoholic. Chemically engineered from birth to drink too much, sleep too little. Perhaps this place, this mindless work, these chemicals, added to his weight. The doctors prescribed all kinds of drugs to take away the edge, but the inborn chemicals won out. I'm nowhere near that point, but there are days I pass by the park. I completed a Master's Degree last fall, and a summer job driving a fork lift, slinging chemicals, doing yardwork to put myself through school, has turned out to be full-time work for part-time pay. There is good news—even though I've worked here five years, my paycheck still lists me as "temporary part-time."

We get thirty minutes for lunch, enough time to dash down the interstate for fast food loaded with additives, preservatives, burgers with bits of gristle and bone, wilted, brown lettuce with traces of pesticide, mayonnaise with a crust from standing open in a Freon chill, grease soaked French fries and onion rings, washed down with diluted caffeine in a wax-covered paper cup. It's the summer of mad cow disease, but if you've seen the chicken and fish or examined the sneeze guard at the salad bar, then it hardly seems madness to eat the beef. All the same, we cry out for irradiated meat. All we need is more chemicals.

Even if I didn't work here, I would support this place, not because of the horror stories I've heard of the days before the new owner took over, when someone would get sprayed or smash a finger at least once a week, the days before OSHA and "175 Days Without an Accident" became a coveted placard, before weekly safety meetings, and a Director of Associate's Safety. The days before talk of clean air, clean water. Before recycling became habit. I'd support this place because I buy chemicals—gasoline and bleach, antifreeze and abrasives. I'm covered in soap, cologne, deodorant, eye drops, contact lenses. I buy can goods and produce, ink pens and paper. 1,001 products made with plastic. In short, I'm a consumer. There's a place in my mind where I exist without a dependency on products of any kind, but I can see no way to get out of this lifestyle, this job, this city, this plastic umbrella. There really is no twelve-step program for chemical dependency of this magnitude.

This place can be peaceful at times. I've poured cement at 6:15 a.m., had a full body sweat by 6:30, stayed as late as 9:00 p.m. with spray adhesive, labels, and shrink wrap, loading trucks by floodlight. I've worked the night shift, solo, from 6:00 p.m. to a.m., mainlining coffee. I've worked New Year's Day in the rain. Worked Saturdays in February on a mezzanine, where we stopped every thirty minutes to beat our hands in a heated storeroom to kill the numb. Time and a half is a drug. But sometimes, the work just plain wears out, and we follow the shade around the plant-like cattle. Your only job is to look busy or hide, so a supervisor doesn't find some task you both know is bullshit. Sometimes, I hide in the maintenance area, talk to guys who weld and listen to talk radio, or grab the keys to the company truck, get in some windshield time, running errands around town, visiting hardware stores. But days like today, when even talking would be too much of a chore, I wander out to my truck, slip a novel in my boot, and walk quickly to the back of the plant. We store rows of chemicals in drums, four to a pallet, stacked two high in the far corner on a concrete slab. There's an alley of sorts behind this row of drums, lined with trees. I often lean up against the cool side of a drum, take off my hard hat and safety glasses, sometimes even my boots, and read for an hour or more. We've all got our secret hiding places to read in, sleep, or just sit and think. Watch squirrels run along the top of the chain-link fence, trying to figure a way to escape.

The intercom finds you anywhere, and the speaker blares my name. Reading cut short. I grab my garb and slip around the rows of drums, down the concrete ramp. A page usually means spill clean-up, an errand to run, a wrench to hold, but today it's a phone call. My wife. She's found a house for rent. Forty miles east of town. We've lived inside paper-thin walls for eight years. Rented rooms. Wife-beaters throwing spouses and lamps down steps. Brothers beating the hell out of one another in the parking lot. Slashed tires and stolen plates. Guys peeing in bushes. Loud music and squeaking bed springs. It's time to get out. But this sounds out. Forty miles. I'm leaving work early. Gotta see this.

The house looks like it was built in a ditch. Dirty yellow with black aluminum shutters. Metal front door, too hot to touch. The house faces west. Inside, there's a combination of worn, dingy carpet and Seventies-looking tile. Brown wood spiders in every room. There's no grass in the yard. Fire ant mounds everywhere. Overall, I'd say it's a sad, hot house in need of paint and poison. Yet, to get here, we traveled a mile down a two-lane blacktop road, lined with trees. The nearest houses are a half-mile away. Nothing but Mesquites and Pines, cattle and barbed wire in all directions.

I stand in the road to get the panoramic view. It's not much, so I shut my eyes and listen. I take a deep breath—no fast food smell, car exhaust, or chemical plants. No highway hum of eighteen-wheelers, horn blasts, kids crying. No generators, radios, airplanes, or car alarms. There are sounds I can imagine—coffee beans grinding, percolating slowly, a screen door slam with me on the back porch, cup in hand at sunrise. I open my eyes—before me is not a dream house, not even something I would own, but it feels like something we should do. This halfway house for the chemically dependent.

BEGINNER'S LUCK

Twenty-thousand bees could have been waiting on my porch, a sixty-thousand dollar loan hanging on the line, and I work forty miles from home, so I was driving eighty-five, a book open on my lap called, *You and Your New Hive*, trying to memorize sugar to water ratios, trying to visualize how to feed the bees with a paint brush through the cage in a light dabbing motion so I wouldn't sever their tongues, crunching numbers in my head according to what the banker said about the percentage they would loan based on what our bank book read, hoping like hell the bees weren't dead (*they'll be starving from the trip, once they arrive by mail*), that my parent's check had cleared (*due to holds on your account, your available amount...*), that the cop around the corner (*may I see your license, please?*), would understand I had to be back at work by 1:00, which gave me seven minutes for the bees, seven minutes to call the bank, one minute to wash an apple and grind my truck into reverse, taking a deep breath while finding first before it hurled me down the road again.

The fast lane ruins the ease of driving, keeps you looking in the rear for objects rushing to overtake you, forcing the decision—do I hold my fleeting ground, white-knuckled and alert, or edge to the side, hug the yellow line, behind cattle trucks and old ladies on their way to market

THE RISK INVOLVED

place? The slow lane removes the tension of the onslaught bearing down, and there's no need for mirrors because you've examined everything: you know for certain it was a dead possum, not a dog about to dart; a stalled white Buick, not a cop ready to give chase; a man called crazy Larry, dragging a cross on wheels, not at all something to stop for, not at all something to fear. The slow lane gives permission to dwell upon the past, to watch where you are going, and be content with where you are.

The windshield becomes your world, but one's perspective can be lost, trapped in alluring boxes, like televisions, movie screens, or peeking through the key hole of an historic two-story home whose blue face has been lifted with fresh paint and white trim, a new tin roof waiting for rain that lasts all through the night, which Christa and I did one Easter Sunday after seeing it was for sale. Peeking through the keyhole, visualization is the key—the ability to see things not yet present, to overlook the things that are. Tunnel vision reveals a spot on the far wall of the room, a rose-patterned piece of paper, seen through dust-swirled light—the dangerous hue of memory, so strong it knocks you back to a place where you agree *this is what we're looking for*, sends you rushing 'round the corner, beneath a line of pecan trees, shells crunching with every step, to peer into a window framed by ceilings fifteen foot high, sliding doors dividing rooms, transoms and hardwood floors.

What windows don't reveal is dry glue spirals along the floor where carpet was laid to stave off cold due to lack of insulation, burrowed termites making tracks, black grout and shifting tile, water stains in every room, molded plaster above the sink, the horror behind the stove, and enough crevices and cracks to make a highway map. What you don't see is copper wire that runs throughout the house.

To see these things, you've got to meet the owner with the key, but even with the door unlocked, one's vision can be blurred by one simple, spoken word—*potential*. We made lists, divided into things we'd want and things we'd need. I imagined hanging sheetrock but kept returning to the scene of split thumbnails, busted corners, pieces falling on my head. I could feel the rented sander moving smoothly across the floor, but the back pain, taste of sawdust, stench of burnt wood, made me weak. I saw trips to local merchants, making small talk checking out, collecting tips on home improvements, bits of wisdom from old men, but return trips to take back shower kits, mismatched bolts and nuts and screws, the wrong shade of nearly everything kept me awake at night. We talked money with our parents, with the bankers, with our friends, but in the end our conversations added up to this: we'd be in debt for thirty years to most everyone we knew; we'd be tired, poor, frustrated, and possibly divorced, so we left this perfect pit for some other couple's money, returned to our rent house with a different point of view. We have just enough knowledge of how to "do it yourself" to do ourselves great damage beyond anyone's repair.

The ceiling is hopeless as you focus through a latticework of light, fingers locked down over eyes while you're lying on the couch, a *Home Buyer's Guide for Morons* open on your chest, pressing that lack of understanding deep into your ribs. It's astounding just how little eighty-thousand bucks can buy, but we're in our twenties, no life savings, two liberal arts degrees—good Americans whose reach always exceeds our grasp. A starting point is key, a foundation on which to build, so after the disappointment of the hundred-year-old house, our list of what we wanted was narrowed down to this: a house still in the country, though we both worked in the city. We were never moving back there. We had simplified our lives.

We drove down dirt roads following leads of "must see to appreciate" and "a fixer upper's dream" with landmarks as our guide, rather than street signs. We passed trailer parks and prisons, unappreciative of our dreams, and on arrival at most locations, Christa whispered, "turn around." Cocks raised for fighting, a herd of goats and several hogs, a myriad of ostriches seemed to be the pets of choice for any prospective neighbors in the places we could afford. The livestock itself was not offensive, but we're talking half-acre lots. I had envisioned a rural paradise without the petting zoo. Twenty-three houses in three weeks and we never left the car.

THE RISK INVOLVED

You can't tell much about a house in two inches of black and white, but one afternoon we ditched the lists the realtor kept cranking out for an ad: "Great starter home. Three bedrooms, one bath. Cathedral ceiling in the living room. Wooden floors and carpet. Separate laundry and workshop," and the line that reeled me in, "within walking distance of a lake." *Starter home* suggests a place you plan to leave once you get promoted, your numbers hit, or someone dies. Folks don't measure rainfall at a starter home, or record floodwaters by marks on a fence post, or remember the longest dry spell, or hottest summer on the place. They don't know when the first frost hits or when it's safe to plant, and they're not likely to plant shrubs, perennials, or trees. A starter home seems to be a place where people just kill time until their lives begin. I wanted more than a start, so I drove the ten miles east; left the highway; passed large fields of cattle, corn, and pecan trees; wound up a large incline; coasted down a narrow road into a small community spread out nearby a lake. We stopped in front of the house and actually got out of the car.

Introspection becomes more painful once you decide you want a house. How many problems someone is leaving do you really want to buy? But this one was in our budget, and we were tired of the search, so we made an offer that they countered, which we accepted and returned, contingent on the mortgage company and an inspector's fine-toothed comb. He tested sockets, checked for termites, shook his head at the breaker box, while I inspected six large windows in the living room alone, Texas star above the mantle, wooden panel and beadboard. He pulled up carpet, climbed into the attic, ran the water, checked the pipes, while I picked out office space and imagined book-lined shelves. We moved through the house in silence, each making a list—his was written, checking off everything done wrong; mine was mental, justifying everything that could be right. The realization began to creep as I followed him to the porch, berries beneath our feet from two trees growing through the boards, that I wouldn't buy a horse because I'm no good judge of teeth, so why the hell was I pretending I knew how to buy a house?

JEFFREY UTZINGER

"I thought you told me this was foundation," he said, donning overhauls and baseball cap. I had guessed and only then realized the house was pier and beam. "If I see a spider or snake, the underworld excursion is over." This sounded reasonable, so I helped tear away a piece of fiberglass, one of many, that were screwed like a skirt around the house. Handed him his flashlight, wished him luck, and watched his rubber boots disappear. Distinguishing shapes in near darkness, giving a shadow a sharp edge, maybe eyes and fangs and muzzle can be frightening when you're a child, and I returned to these faint nightmares while imagining the creatures hidden beneath the house. It's a relief once you're older to learn one can rationalize away fear, but imagination can still wreak havoc when you find yourself on uncertain ground. I walked the perimeter of the acre, marked by a short stone wall over pea gravel and dirt, interspersed with weeds, but I counted nineteen live oak trees, two more that were dead, a mimosa and two fruit trees, fourteen crepe myrtles that lined the road, and countless cedar stumps and scrubs that were scattered all throughout. I felt the chainsaw's rough vibration as I laid dead trees on a dime. The crunching of a chipper sending mulch across the lawn. Then lying in a hammock looking through a latticework of leaves, even in winter with bare branches, an orange sky falling down, and at nighttime with stars on black limbs like illuminated leaves.

There are forces that seem to pull me farther into the woods, farther to the northeast than we had planned to move. Perhaps a slow migration back to where I was born, but the northern tip of Kentucky is still nine hundred miles away. I've lived in Texas twice as long as I ever lived in that place, married a girl from Louisiana, and had a full-time job, on the verge of purchasing a house with a little land—not exactly the blueprints for moving home again. The house, though, seemed akin to what I remembered of those ten years, and the longer I looked around, the more I knew I had to stay.

Storage buildings fanned like moons around the backside of the house, a laundry room outside the back door, a walk-in shed to its right, another in the side yard with a door only waist high. The workshop, though, clinched the deal—a miniature of the house, painted gray with white trim, complete with its own tin roof. I walked off a rough measurement, twenty feet by twelve, more space than I could use for storage, than I could use for anything. The windows were thick with cobwebs, sawdust, a layer of dirt. I rubbed a circle with my elbow just to peer inside—there was lumber, cabinets, tables, bicycles, and tools, filled almost top to bottom, and I wondered what would be left behind. I cleared my mind of clutter, envisioned standing in the room, near empty save for a worktable on which sat a piece of wood, measured and pencil-marked, the saw's teeth on the line. I could hear the high-pitched whine as the blade sliced through the wood, the cut piece dropping to the floor, raising a cloud of dust. I'm not sure what I was building, but it felt like something good.

I could have been disturbed by the message the inspector bore when he emerged from beneath the house, and we went over his checklist. Nothing passed inspection, but this didn't mean a thing since we were in the country, except that several beams were twisted, hence the slant of the kitchen floor, others needed bracing, which was why it was hard to close some doors, termites had done damage, and the dishwasher drained, along with the hot water heater, straight to the ground, the shower head and sinks all leaked, and the tin roof had been screwed flush to the old shingles—the perfect combination for moisture accumulation, an unstable foundation, and lots of expensive repairs. Fortunately, I'm in the habit of ignoring sound advice, so I figured we could live with too few outlets, the absence of dead bolts, the possibility of poor wiring, the threat of flood and theft and fire, and all because of this: I had covered every inch of ground, both inside and out, and had seen what I'd be doing once we were living here. Those of us who have been scattered (and that's most of us these days), who long for a sense of place, sometimes have to settle for a place they can afford.

JEFFREY UTZINGER

❦ ❦ ❦

Preparation is the key in major life decisions, making smooth transitions, allowing one's self to be transformed, but I prefer baptism by fire, learn and burn as you go. Paperwork makes me nervous, the filling out of forms, careful planning and equations, lists that separate your choices into black and white. I'm easily distracted, so in the midst of searching for a home, a friend mentioned he once kept bees, and I decided to build a hive. When I proposed it to Christa, she readily agreed, so I began reading up on apiculture, four books in a month, in between plowing through the pages on how to buy a house. I faxed and phoned loan officers, exterminators, banks, electricians and realtors, my parents and close friends. Joined a beekeeper's association, bought a bottom board, brood box, nine frames of wax foundation, and a telescoping top. Listened to frustrated explanations of escrow and equity, filled out forms on our finances, made a stab at our net worth. Borrowed a smoker, and a bee suit from a couple who lived nearby. Was told I needed two house payments in the bank at all times. Told I needed to move slowly, and to learn to sing to bees.

The postmaster called one morning, sounding nervous, at 6:00 a.m. Two pounds of bees sat on his counter with a label bearing my name. We were on our way to work, but I promised I'd be there by noon. I picked them up, made sugar syrup, brushed it onto the cage, shut them in the bathroom to ward off curious cats, made a quick call to the banker who told me our loan had been approved, and rushed back to the city sixty-thousand dollars in debt but on my way to raising sixty-thousand bees.

That night I had the smoker burning hot after two or three false starts; it sent curls of smoke to snake around my boots, the tops of which were bonded to the legs of my jump suit, wrapped six times with duct tape—no bees were getting in. Zipper tight from crotch to voice box, collar snapped and bee veil on. Leather gloves stretched to the elbows, elastic bands around the top. I raised a flat-head screwdriver to Christa standing by in t-shirt, shorts, and sandals, snapping pictures of each step. There is so much that could go wrong when hiving a package of bees. It's best to watch an experienced hand before trying it yourself, but somewhere in my youth, after reading Emerson and Thoreau, I got the notion that it's un-American to ask anyone for help. I had the illustrated summary from *The Beginner Beekeeper's Guide* that I kept open near my feet, but it's near impossible to read through a bee veil, so the mistakes I made along the way are what pictures never show.

Crucial bits of information are often neglected in a text, such as what one's supposed to do if there's no queen cage to be found. It's supposed to be suspended with a wire from the top, but when I pried open the lid and removed the empty feeder, I was greeted only by the hum of hungry worker bees. They had been doused with water, so at least they didn't fly as my fingers disappeared into the soggy mass. My hand sunk to the bottom as they closed around my wrist, but I couldn't feel a single leg through the leather gloves. Finally, my thumb and index finger closed around a solid form, and I freed the tiny cage, held it toward my face, but my view was still obstructed by a thick blanket of bees, who by instinct, or by habit, had clustered around the queen. I flung my arm downward in a quick snapping motion, sending the clinging bees back to the ground; a few found the cage, but I was beginning to feel anxious, so I closed up the lid. A queen cage is roughly the size of a harmonica, with two identical circles carved out of the sides. One holds the queen with several attendants. The other holds a sugar cube. Commercial queens are reared separate from the workers, so there's no guarantee they'll accept each other in the hive. Her scent becomes familiar while traveling through the mail, and the workers feel her body through the thin, black mesh. There's a cork on either end, pencil-eraser size, and the workers will chew through once the cork is removed. This takes several days which provides more of a chance the subjects will accept her rule once the queen is free.

JEFFREY UTZINGER

Another bit of information I hadn't seen, in text or illustration, was how one went about dislodging the wooden cork. I used a screwdriver to prod and push, but the head was the same size, so I moved the tip toward a staple that held the thin mesh tight to wood. The staple popped out since the wood was wet from the soaking I'd given the bees, and the screwdriver skimmed right under the screen, plowed through the sugar, and demolished a bee. Queen's bodies are longer, so I should have been able to tell if I'd severed her head, but my vision was blurred by the veil and a black, surging rage, along with bees who had dried and were beginning to fill the air. I spiked the screwdriver, posed for a picture, suspended the cage at the top of the hive, pretending I hadn't just committed insecticide.

The next step was the only one that had struck me as violent as I read, but it was the perfect follow-up to the mess that I had made. I dropped the box from waist level, and the scattered bees fell to the bottom in one soggy clump, then standing over the brood box, I shook them lightly and watched as they oozed downward, covering the frames. The process was repeated until most were inside. I replaced the cover, set the cage next to the hive, so the stragglers could find the entrance before the sun went down.

Christa went to bed, so I grabbed a lawn chair and a beer. Watched a few bees check out their new porch by moonlight. Waiting can make you crazy, but I couldn't open the hive for two weeks or more to see if they were drawing foundation or if the queen was still alive. But that night it didn't seem bad to idly sit with a chorus of frogs drowning out all other sounds. The bees were finally there, and the new house had been bought. Everything was going okay, although not according to plan, but that's the chance you take when you count on beginner's luck.

THE RISK INVOLVED

A halogen lamp lit up the room like a small electric sun, spattered my shadow across the wall that bent at the ceiling's edge, made the roller and brush seem natural growths from the ends of both my arms. I was drinkin' and dancin' alone at night. Hank Jr. on the radio. Scrapin' and tapin' and slingin' the paint—trying to complete the last room in the new house. I painted and moved for ten hours a day for two weeks straight, and the last night, I was just about ready to fall in a heap, cover up in a drop cloth, and be sung to sleep.

My parents had driven home the day before after helping us pack and move and paint. The bedrooms were dark greens and blues when we moved in, so it took three coats to turn them to sugar-cookie yellow, country white, and sky blue. The rest of the house was tackled with off-white and stepladders, long handled rollers for the high ceilings, rolls and rolls of masking tape. I tried to time the shutting off and turning on of the phone, water, electricity but forgot the new house had propane, so we took cold showers the first night. Christa had a month-long class in the city, so weekends were the only time to sign final paperwork with the realtor and bank. She and mom packed up the house while dad and I loaded the U-haul truck. And I've signed check after check after check made out to everyone in town.

I have problems visualizing what my place is in the world, what I'm supposed to be doing, and how I really want to live. James Galvin writes: "It isn't such a bad thing,/ To live in one world forever," and now that we have moved here, I think that's what I want. A deed, a piece of land, walls to paint, and grass to cut doesn't necessarily bind you to a place. Building structures, planting gardens, laying walkways, stretching fence—these things could bring you closer, but I've done them all before. From the time I was fourteen, until I turned twenty-six, most of the money that I earned came from painting other people's houses, landscaping other people's land. And perhaps that is the difference, what really makes a place one's home—when you're willing to do these things without getting paid. Finding one's place takes more than money, turning compost, thin coats of paint, a summer digging carrots, chopping roots, collecting stone. It takes my grandfather's knowledge, dead for twenty years, of every plant and tree that grew upon his land, and my uncle's plow and cattle, the peach and apple grove, grandma's singing in the choir for more than forty years, my mother's records of the weather, down to every inch of rain, my father's woods and rivers that he knew like a street map. The ability to recognize a thousand tracks in mud and dirt and snow.

I returned to the rent house late one evening to find bees spilling from the hive, fanned above the entrance, poured over the ledge, clinging together. Stalactites that hummed. I'd watched for weeks as their numbers increased, relieved that the queen was alive, laying eggs, but anxious about moving them to the new house. My truck sat on the lawn next to the hive as I waited on the tailgate for the sun to go down. Dusk usually means everyone is inside, but it was still ninety degrees, so they were cooling themselves. A new super should have been added, but in the midst of everything else, I'd put off the bees until last.

A warm breeze snuffed out match after match, and scattered oak leaves, mesquite chips, and bits of burnt paper across the dry grass. I would get something lit inside the smoker but add too much fuel and smother the flame. Knock the smoldering pile onto the tailgate, reach for more paper, strike a new match. Certain we wouldn't get back the safety deposit if I set the lawn afire and burned the house down.

Beekeeping may be the closest I ever get to farming—a practice dependent on weather and patience. A little good luck. Fortunate for me, though, it isn't a living because it appears I've still much to learn. Once the smoker was going, the bees moved inside. A few stranglers remained, but I stapled a strip of old window screen across the mouth of the hive, secured the package with pieces of twine, and realized it

THE RISK INVOLVED

was too heavy for one person to move. Of course, I did it anyway, arms wrapped halfway 'round the hive, bent over taking one-inch steps, stray bees pelting my veil. The hive slammed into the tailgate when I tried to push it in. I teetered backward, cursing, and on the second try, caught just enough of the corner to rest it on the ledge. Bees clustered around the entrance on the wrong side of the screen. I crushed a few while pushing, brushed a few more off my sleeves. The heat was overwhelming, even though the sun was gone. I grabbed the cement blocks and wedged in the hive. Jumped into the truck, drove with windows up to prevent any intrusions from angry bees along the way.

Unloading them was easier than getting them onto the truck. I used a wheelbarrow to cart them out back, but when I checked the next morning to see how they'd adjusted, not a single bee could be seen on the ledge or in the air. We only moved ten miles away, but somewhere along the trip, they must have decided they didn't want to leave the old place. Heat, overcrowding, or perhaps the rough movement could have caused them to swarm. Entire colonies seldom leave once they're established, but I couldn't bear to open the cover to see if any remained. Envisioning them there, or imagining them gone, was easier than verifying either with my own eyes.

My grandfather kept bees, but I never met him. I didn't know that he did until I ordered my hive. Dad told me one night while we were moving that he remembered getting stung on his feet, chewing on comb, how the honey was so sickly sweet. He didn't remember what became of the hives, said they may still be rotting in the sheds back home. The promise of honey, and the time I had spent had nothing to do with the sadness I felt as I walked through the yard listening for bees. The idea that they'd gather nectar from our flowers, pollinate our garden, throw swarms in our trees seemed to be something that could make this place more our home. Give me something in common with my father's father, something I didn't know that I wanted until the bees were gone.

JEFFREY UTZINGER

❦ ❦ ❦

Sawdust, like silt, has settled over everything in the workshop that the previous owner left behind. It clings to the walls and window sills, lines shelves holding misshapen wood, paint, coffee, and beer cans, bottles and boxes, sits in large piles on the floor, separating the things that I brought along—power tools, lawn mower, rakes, hoes, and spades, buckets and the tiller, a few bags of nails. I imagine the previous owner measuring the U-haul, trying to squeeze this work table in between bikes, finding space for loose lumber, justifying taking up room with cans full of bolts, screwdrivers and nails, cursing the sun setting, the trip still ahead, taking one last look, and driving away. Any man who works with his hands would be loathe to leave this space.

Five trash cans, full, lined one of the driveways, along with boxes and buckets overflowing and packed with sawdust and glass, but I'm making my way through each of their contents with leather gloves and the hope I'll find something to keep. A few weeks after I had moved the hive, I was crouched over a large pile of sawdust, carefully running my fingers through, remembering as a boy at dad's company picnic, a similar game searching for coins, but now I'm hoping to find another man's tools. Channel locks had been the greatest reward, but I had a line of coffee cans, sorting screws, nuts, and nails. There was still trim to be painted inside the house, but there was a great satisfaction in organizing the shop, not knowing what mystery I'd uncover next. Getting married, a full-time job, and buying a house, I guess qualifies you as becoming an adult. Yet it struck me how little I had changed if I could still be entertained with ten penny nails, wood shavings, and cans.

My thoughts were interrupted by an insect buzz. Florescent lightbulbs hung down from the ceiling, and something kept dropping to the worktable and spinning before taking off back to the light. I stood to look closer but already knew the honeybee's hum. One's wings flickered madly; she was down on her back, making spirals in sawdust, making my heart beat fast. I threw open the shed's back doors. The hive sat a few feet away, undisturbed since the morning I'd thought they had fled. I removed the cover, and there was just enough light to see a dozen or so bees moving along the foundation. They could have been feral, bees who came across an empty hive, or stragglers from the original, too stubborn to leave, but worker bees have no purpose, and never live long if there's not a queen present, and more than two weeks had passed. I shut the lid slowly and returned to my work, humming softly and listening to bees buzz the light. I wanted to tell them their main task should be to build up the hive, but we all take false trails, wrong turns, and dead ends. The key is to keep working until you find your way home.

THE RISK INVOLVED

We run a moonshiner's risk down Highway 71, a fifty-mile stretch of road between our house in Indian Lake and Austin, Texas where we work; a risk of being pinched by cops for expired inspection stickers, careless handling of toxins, reckless driving, excessive speed. Antifreeze leaks from my wife's blue Ford through a pinhole-laden radiator at the rate of one gallon per every three days. Christa draws water from a milk jug she keeps in the backseat, every time the needle leans too far to hot. My red Ford is a tanker, leaving oil slicks in its wake. The dashboard illumined by the "check oil" light and the toolbox crammed tight with spent quart containers and oil residue. We gun hell for rubber, fifteen miles through winding unlit roads to hit the highway. Christa leaves before sunup; I return at sundown. Coming and going, day in and day out, one hundred and twenty miles. Round trip. Odometers spin two hundred and forty miles onto two Fords with a combined mileage of two-hundred-sixty-thousand miles. Fifty-four gallons of gas and two quarts of oil a week. One might question the wisdom of burning this much rubber, coming home this exhausted, driving oneself crazy just for a job. Just so we can live among live oak and scorpions, keep bees, plant gardens, turn compost, walk to a lake. Just so we can say, on weekends and vacations, we have gotten away from it all.

THE RISK INVOLVED

Pinhole leaks kill you slowly, like a crack in a dam—you know the danger is coming, but you think you have time. Fix it tomorrow, next week, next month, when there's more time and more money. When there's money at all. We were catching our breath in the eye of a storm. Plugging leaks with the proof we were financially sound: pink slips from two vehicles finally paid off, check carbons chronicling first-year house payments, receipts for home improvements and repairs, and a collection of stubs from two full-time jobs, complete with deductions sent to Uncle Sam. In this flutter of paper and time logged on asphalt, an image of a boat sailed through my daydreams, cut and tacked me through traffic, helped me drift asleep every night. I'd thumb idly through ads in the local paper, but everything for sale was too big, too new, too over-priced. The image was ten feet, two man, flat bottom, aluminum, with a small trolling motor and trailer, an anchor and live well.

Christa spotted an ad in the Austin paper for "Captain Jack's Used Fishing Boats & Repair," so we drove down a road in far east Del Valle, two lanes, pocked with pot holes, lined with spontaneous dumps of sofas, exploding trash bags, Styrofoam and stray dogs, made a sharp left at a bend into a lot full of shipwrecked vessels in weeds. A pit bull on a log chain kept our course tight toward a shack—part business, part homestead, wholly askew. A second hound of indeterminate breed and unbelievable filth trotted silent around a trailer, poked us through a doorway minus its door. *The worst day of fishing is better than the best day of work* hung more like a warning of what we'd receive if we sounded the bell perched on the counter inside. We sounded it lightly to rouse Captain Jack from the boxes and motors and tackle and twine. When no one appeared, I suggested we leave, but Christa wanted to look around outside.

The mongrel was gone, and pit bull asleep when we emerged and gravitated toward an enormous carport, tall as a two-story house, tin-covered and open at one end as though the plywood, Plexiglas, gears, chains, and bottles spilling from its mouth had exploded the fourth wall.

A high-pitched drill and mambo music wafted from inside. We stood at the entrance staring down a ski boat, suspended halfway from the ceiling with chain, its nose resting on blocks. A man perched on the side in shadows cast from a halogen lamp overhead. He whacked the boat's side with a monkey wrench and Captain Jack's head, complete with a blonde shock of hair, and Black and Tan cigar appeared over the hull.

"See anything ya like?"

"We just got here."

"Well, look around. Everything's $500. Cash. We'll load. You haul."

"Does anything actually run?" Christa asked.

Jack smiled. Blew smoke. Held his hand out toward his first mate without looking, as the wrench was placed in his hand.

"I can get you a trolling motor. $150. Cash. Boats are a little worn, but they float. Most got a live well that make great coolers. Can see you now."

The Captain's head disappeared.

"Tooling 'round. Drinking beer. Catching bass," echoed from inside the boat.

I could see myself too, but not in a Captain Jack wreck. We slogged through tall weeds, our pants dewed to the knees, cockleburs clinging, looking for ticks, wove through aisles, hopping aboard, teetering, stamping, ruling every choice out. Boats too big for any trolling motor I'd seen, faded and cracked, sun-rotted and ripped, molded, broken seats in every color, size, and style. I began to imagine Captain Jack surveying a craggy coast, waiting for hapless travelers to capsize. Twenty minutes and forty boats passed without possibility, so we wound our way back to the car disappointed but relieved that we were neither snake nor spider bitten. We left without bidding adieu to Jack and his mate.

The boat search continued half-hearted a week after our escape from Captain Jack's. This time a few miles from home. This time a place that sold *exactly what you want* and turned out to have exactly what I wanted: six foot, ten foot, twelve foot and twenty, flat bottom, aluminum, shiny and green. We pulled through a chain-link fenced gravel lot, were met by a young woman in khaki shorts, blue t-shirt, who led us to the boats lined on cement blocks, chained with bright silver links on close-trimmed grass. Followed into the shop with rows of clearly marked boxes, picture side out, of trolling motors, horsepower finely lettered in black ink. We perused colored brochures, slick and enticing, even let her add numbers on her desk calculator, complete with two possible payment plans for ten feet, one motor and trailer, tax, title, and license, took her card with the totals, her numbers and name.

"Well, that was fun."

"You've got to get a better job."

"Or drink cheaper beer."

"Or fish from the dam."

"Or eat what I catch."

"Or jump in a lake."

My window of opportunity was shrinking to pinhole size. Both Fords were fading fast, and the race was on to see which would go first. The pastoral image peeled with each passing mile, revealing how much damage unattended leaks and cracks can do. The risk involved in leaving late adolescence behind, in hitching one's wagon to another human's star, in trading everything you're worth for wood, plaster, and plumbing covered with tin, in seeking finely carved furniture to fill empty spaces, in power tool investments, in scanning plastic with the promise you'll pay for everything one day, in surrendering to the tick of the full-time time clock, and growing into the phrase "responsible adult" is this: you have to start using your head.

Mine was turned, once again, on the way home from fishing at Christa's grandmother's farm. Twenty miles of blacktop county roads, lined with nothing but scattered houses and churches; forests, fields, and farms lie between grandma's house and ours. Great opportunity to lay open a truck that has lately taken to jolts and stalls at uneven speeds. I'd topped seventy-five, rattling toward eighty, when what I'd been searching for passed by in a blur. Wedged between a gated gravel drive and a stand of mesquite trees sat a boat with a for sale sign tacked to the side. I made a wild loop in the road and pulled into the ditch, wrote down the number and drove home.

"I'm callin' about the boat."

"Waterproof as a duck's ass."

"How much?"

"Comes with a twenty-five horsepower engine, trolling motor, trailer, battery, and oar. $550 cash."

"$550?"

"The gas is the can is free."

"I'll ask the wife. Call you back."

I yelled from the bedroom. Didn't want to see Christa's expression.

"See if he'll come down."

I'd rather negotiate a fishhook from my thumb than haggle about a price, but $550 could go a long way in keeping one of the cars on the road. I felt the pinhole shrinking and re-dialed the phone.

"Just called about the boat. Wife wants to know if you'll take $500."

"I'll ask the wife. Call you back."

I yelled from the bedroom. Didn't want to see Christa's expression.

"I offered five hundred."

"Why not four?"

"Did I mention it comes with an oar?"

"An oar. Yeah, great."

The phone rang.

"You called about the boat. The wife says okay."

Trappings of a shady deal surrounded the exchange. The land where the boat was stranded didn't belong to the man, but he could be there in twenty minutes. Christa and I were there in ten, waiting in the ditch down a stretch of road where a parked car either meant it was abandoned or in distress, wondering if we could transfer money in time to cover the hot check we were about to pass. The man arrived moments later, bolt cutters in hand; he'd forgotten the combination, and as he clipped the chain that held the vessel to a tree, he explained he was in a hurry, had a family gathering to attend, but he'd agreed to the price and the exchange this afternoon because though he loved fishing, he no longer had the time, and what the boat lacked in looks, he added, flipping off a tarp weighed down by rotted leaves, it made up in strength. I took his words hook, line, and sinker, squelching the thought that I was being taken down the river in an old, stolen boat.

A boat that's ten feet of aluminum, repellant to all paint, save the stubborn streaks of cedar green. Halved by a live well covered in plywood attached by thin hinges. A flat aluminum seat in the stem and stern. Fifteen feet of rope tied to the bow with a sliding clip on the end to hold the anchor fast. The anchor itself is a bell-shaped piece of metal welded to a rusted handle and ring, filled with concrete. Gas-powered engine perched on the rear, held tight with two screw clamps.

"It looks dirty," Christa said, as we waved to the man, eased onto the road. The ball hitch I had was too large, so we tied the trailer to my bumper with twine. Drove twenty miles an hour home.

"Yeah, just about perfect," I said.

The boat hadn't been used in years, so I pulled the motor, laid it to rest on the workshop table. Shined a flashlight in the opening of the gas can after prying the lid off with a screwdriver. Bits of dry-rotted gasket floated in a primer red liquid that I would later use to burn stumps. I squeezed the plastic bulb connected to the can; gas oozed from hoses attached to either end. The bulb itself split on the underside. As promised, though, a battery and trolling motor lay in the boat; the positive wire connection frayed. I clipped the respective clamps onto the posts, resulting in not so much as a spark. Jumping a lawn- and tractor-size battery with my truck seemed a poor idea. The bonus oar was three feet long, made of sun-bleached plastic. I dug my nail into the handle, desperate to be on water. Began to wonder if we should have asked for a receipt of some kind. Examined the boat itself for any visible holes and came across an expired registration sticker. Began to wonder if you could get one renewed with no proof of purchase. If fishing boats had titles. Finally decided that sometimes buying a little peace of mind is a risk. Sometimes you have to jump right in. Get your feet wet.

Indian Lake is fed by a natural spring on its north side and dammed two miles south, making it little more than a sprawling pond. East to west is half a mile wide, give or take a dock or cove. Surrounded by trees and houses. A steady wind blows from the northeast from just after sunrise to an hour or so before sunset, shifting direction and intensity throughout the day, from season to season; but my first afternoon with a boat, it was sharp, making caps on the surface, rolling small waves onto the boat ramp that's wedged at the base of the dam.

The last attempt I'd made backing a trailer had been three years before when I worked at a chemical plant. My hands had grown soft. My maneuvering skills dulled. Christa made emphatic motions with one hand, while trying to keep the hair out of her face with the other, and I zigged the boat into zags until one tire of the trailer rested on the cement ramp, the other hanging over the edge. Close enough to drop. The gear was rusted, but I popped the handle back, flipped the latch to release the tension, and the boat slid down the rollers and slipped into the water, still fastened to the nylon strap. The wind whipped it into a group of cattails, so I kicked off my shoes and, waist deep in water, pushed the boat to the other side of the trailer, where it rested perpendicular to the shore. I unclipped the nylon strap and handed Christa the rope, while I pulled the trailer from the water and parked the truck. I'd considered bringing a beer to christen the boat, but before naming and ceremony, I figured I should see if it would float.

Christa sat in the middle, hands gripped tight to the sides, while I pushed the boat, bottom scraping, my feet sinking in soft mud. "Lean left," I warned as I passed on the right, settled into the back and began to row. The initial kick hurled us from shore, but the wind sent us into a spin despite my furious rowing, alternating sides, splashing us both.

THE RISK INVOLVED

We came to rest against the cattails, laughing and wet, until the wind died long enough for me to paddle back toward the center of the lake. Gusts kept sending us back to shore, back to the cattails, or toward a man sitting bemused on his dock trying to fish. My arms finally gave out, and Christa got bored, so we conceded defeat, drifted to a halt in the mud and returned home. The rush had lasted a second but was worth five hundred dollars—that moment when my foot on dry land had lifted and I was standing stork-like, looking down, the boat rushing forward, water rushing backward, and I hunched down to center my weight, avoid the capsize, and grabbed the oar before the wind blew us back to shore. The exhilaration of escape. The risk of being brought down.

I'd needled the pinhole, picked and gouged until the trickle became a stream, and the opening became a waterway large enough to drive a fishing boat through. I bought two six-foot, wooden-lacquered oars, bothered a little man in a blue vest to use his metal hook to retrieve two bright orange life jackets from a row that hung like garland near the ceiling; picked out a second battery exactly the same as the one the man had given me, a battery charger so that I'd always have back up, an inch and a quarter trailer hitch, a roll of fishing line, bags of hooks, boxes of sinkers, a float and a carton of live worms—all which brought the boat-buying adventure closer to the six hundred dollar mark. Then the Fords broke down; first the blue, then the red.

There's risk involved in getting away from it all, and if you're going to drive your vehicles into the ground, practice sporadic maintenance, live an hour from work, half an hour from any store, then it might be helpful to know a thing or two about car repairs. The blue Ford jerked and lurched Christa home one Friday night; she delivered the news mid-twist through my second beer. I drove to the lake and back, to the main road and back, *around* the lake and back, full beer between my legs to serve as a liquid seismograph. Didn't spill a drop. Car glitches are like landing a five-pound bass: they seldom occur when there's anyone else to confirm. We lit out late Saturday morning for a second test drive, venturing toward the Wal-Mart thirty miles away. The car sputtered, about fifteen miles out, just as I accelerated to merge onto the highway, and died completely as I coasted onto the shoulder.

"That what you meant about it jerking?"

"What'd you do?"

"Just drove the car."

"But you did something. It never died on me."

"Yes, that's helpful."

"Get out and see if you can tell what's wrong."

It's a game we play: she pretends she's a nagging wife. I pretend I can fix things with my hands. And so, I popped the hood, made sure the oil cap was screwed tight, wiggled the battery cables, and did the walkaround, kicking the tires for good measure. Mainly for the benefit of the cars rushing by.

"Yeah, I have no idea," I announced, crawling inside.

"You wanna walk home?"

"Yeah, me neither."

The risk involved in getting away from it all is you might get stranded, and if you don't carry cell phones, you'd better carry quarters, or wear good walking shoes. At the very least, you should get to know your neighbors, so you'll have someone to call if you ever make it to a phone. Since we'd done none of the above, we watched cars and trucks blow by on business or pleasure from Houston to Austin and back again. Acknowledging our plight by changing lanes or swerving slightly. The leery and the rushed. Finally, a local man slowed on his way to his daughter's house. Didn't have time to backtrack us to Indian Lake, but he was glad to take us west. Moving in the wrong direction seemed better than sitting still. Midway between the town where we live and the next town over is a place called Alum Creek—a hodgepodge of slanting buildings and old houses where people sell antiques. Christa's favorite place to visit on Saturday afternoons and the source of half the furniture we have around the house. Most of the merchants know her by name, so we had the man drop us there. Not much of a plan—spend the afternoon stranded among semi-friends. Perhaps they'd tire of our browsing and take us home.

Two guys own a shop called The Red Door; our kitchen table, four chairs, buffet, various dishes and knickknacks came from them, so we stopped there first. Not only did the owners lend us their phone, but their truck as well, to run our errands while the car was being towed. It was a small gesture, I suppose, and some would argue, symbiotic, since they'd make up for the wear and tear on their truck through a future sale of another antique. Regardless, it was the first time since we'd moved here that I felt like we were becoming part of this place. Not in the sense it was worth the drive to work each day or that being among trees with a little land near a lake had re-awakened something from my youth—all of that had come the day we had moved here—but in the sense that we belonged among these people, who like us, had "gotten away," or who had the sense from the beginning to stay in the town of their birth.

The feeling lasted until Monday morning found us with one vehicle, Austin bound, running late when we needed to run early to get us both to work on time. Stress level rising with the speedometer's arc. We'd hit a near desolate, thirty-mile stretch of highway when at a full seventy-mile-an-hour tilt, the steering wheel stiffened, and I wrestled the truck to the side of the road.

"What are you doing?"

"It died."

"Just like that?"

"Just like that."

Our momentum carried us along the shoulder toward a gravel drive. I turned the steering wheel hard, let gravity pull us down an incline where we came to rest beside the Pecan Palace—a tent-like structure where pecans, whole or shelled, chocolate-, caramel-, and brown sugar-coated, honey and hot sauce, bird houses, squirrel feeders, and candles are sold. We had visited this place on several occasions, even bought my parents a pecan tree a few years before, but it was too early in the morning, and no one was home. We didn't have to walk to the top of the drive, to scan the horizon, to know there wasn't a single house, gas station, or store within sight. I did a dance around the truck, popped the hood, hopped like mad, pumped the gas, and cranked the key. We waited. I tried again. The engine turned, sputtered, wound down. We waited, and wondered what sin in this life or the past had brought such tremendous bad luck down on our heads. The previous year, in October, the water pump had failed in Christa's car, and the clutch had burned out in my truck. After all the repairs, we had dubbed it "The Year with No Christmas." Now it seemed more sinister, and as we abandoned the truck and headed for the highway, we dubbed it "The Curse of October."

I don't pick up hitchhikers or stop for stranded motorists. A shame, really, that we can't help those in need, but if you let your guard down, you've got to be prepared to lose your head, be sodomized, or end up duct taped in somebody's trunk. As a result, I didn't curse the passing stream of cars. We trudged through long grass, avoiding the soft shoulder—getting mowed down would only make the morning worse. Had we not been dressed for work and about to miss meetings, it would have been a nice morning for a stroll. Late October, no wind, seventy degrees and clear. A ridge lay half a mile away, maybe more; distance is difficult to judge on foot. I knew a Texaco gas station was near and hoped when we crested the ridge, we'd see the star. The urge to kick off shoes and run mad into the woods, abandon the day that lay ahead, the crippled automobiles that lay behind, was strong. Christa gripped my hand as though she could read my mind.

We hadn't walked far when a light blue pickup slowed. White taillights crept back toward us, and an older gentleman in a baseball cap asked if we needed a ride. He admitted he usually didn't stop for folks but figured we didn't look shady. A polite thing to say since I most certainly do. My hair is shaved nearly to the scalp, and lately I've taken to wearing

THE RISK INVOLVED

my moustache long. I'm wiry and gaunt. Had I not been dressed for work, the man would have pegged me for a serial killer a mile away. Of course, my wife is tall and has long blonde hair, a look most men would gladly risk stopping for. The man turned out to be part owner of the Pecan Palace, and he gave us tips for making young trees produce. His brother owned the farm adjacent to the school where Christa taught. She had taken a Special Ed class to see the man's cattle and pigs.

The Texaco indeed was just over the hill, so he dropped us by the payphone and went on his way. We bought coffee and took turns checking into work then called the garage where Christa's car was being fixed. Mike the mechanic said he'd send another tow truck, and we could hitch a ride back to town with him. We started the long haul back to the Pecan Palace, but again a man stopped and offered us a ride. I sat in the back next to an empty child seat. I would have guessed having children would make a man more cautious, or at least more in a rush, but decided it must make him more optimistic about life, or at least, more optimistic than me. The tow truck arrived half an hour later, and we piled into the cab, had the driver drop us at the one rental car place in town.

"Hope your ride didn't leave," the rental car guy said as we passed through the door.

"He was towing our ride."

"I have not a single car to rent, and nothing due in 'til late afternoon."

"We'll wait."

Like we had a choice. We'd left home two hours earlier and only managed to progress less than thirty miles. An hour later, a car was returned. A luxury sedan that needed to be cleaned, but we signed the paper work, took the keys, and set out once again. The risk involved in getting away from it all is that some days it might take four vehicles, a tow truck, and coffee, two dollars' worth of quarters, a gold card, and the kindness of strangers to get you back to the place you're trying to escape.

And some days once you get there, you're not sure you want to leave, to get back into the rental car to wait in the jam to pick up your wife to weave through forty miles, back to the mechanic whose favorite phrase is, "I've got good news, and I've got bad news," but it never matters which he gives you first because you never know which is which. I do know this: never name your price. "The Year with No Christmas," when the clutch on my truck began to grind and finding first and reverse was akin to slamming a wedge with a sledgehammer, I told a mechanic I wasn't sure what was wrong but wasn't going to pay to have it fixed if it was over a thousand bucks. Miraculously, the bill came in just under nine hundred and fifty dollars plus tax. Mike the mechanic had recommended the clutch guy with this glowing accolade: "Two guys in town can do the trick. One guy's shop has a dirt floor; the other's got concrete. You can guess which one's cheaper, and which will do a better job. You get what you pay for." I guess. I also guess you pay most for what you don't know.

And you can tell what my wife and I don't know a mile away. Our exchanges with mechanics sound something like this:

"What kind of sound did it make?"

"Like a raspy ping."

"Like a rusty pong."

"Like a cat coughing up a hair ball."

"But drier."

"It might just be pot holes."

"It might be the weather."

"It might cost you an arm but no more than a leg."

The night we pulled into Mike the mechanic's, fifteen minutes before the whistle blew, we weren't feeling hostile. Surviving a day up shit creek sans paddle tends to make one humble and almost grateful that with a little time and money, somebody can get you out of a jam. We'd bought new treads for the car a few weeks before, so Mike remembered us. Remembered we had no kids, like he and his wife, and that we were all happy that way. That we liked Mexican food and had agreed there was only one place in town. We almost felt like friends there in the florescent light, amongst the smell of rubber, scorched coffee and grease. A friendship of convenience, no doubt, but it had been a long day. We were happy to see Mike the mechanic, even though neither car was ready. Happy, even though we waited for nearly an hour after a day that had been comprised of nothing but waiting. Happy, almost, that something had gone awry so that we could give him our money. That warm-happy-the-mechanic-is-great feeling lasted until Mike gave us the signal and handed us the key.

"The radiator in the blue car was shot, so we replaced it."

"Great. What about the truck?"

"It started as soon as the tow truck dropped it off. We've driven it around all day and can't find anything wrong."

"Oh."

"You want to leave it here one more day?"

"Sure. We'll be fine with one car."

"Well, Bud just took the blue car for a spin and said it jerked a bit."

"That's what we said when we had it towed in."

"Oh." We all stopped smiling in unison. Mike the mechanic read the notes he'd made. Christa and I stole a sideways glance. Half expected an anchor from a nightly news program to reveal the hidden microphone. Reveal the scandal of automotive repair.

"Yes. Once we got to looking at it, the radiator was so bad, we thought we'd found the problem."

"Would that make it shake?"

"It could."

"Did it? In this case?"

"It's probably spark plugs. Bring it back tomorrow. Just wanted you to have a car."

I'm an optimist in many ways, wanting to believe the most simple solution is always the key, and so Tuesday morning on our trek back to Austin, I bought new spark plugs and plug wires. Self-made man does it himself. Christa had a conference in El Paso, so I drove her to the hotel to meet a group of friends who had rented a van to take the five-day trip. As we pulled into the parking lot, the car jerked and sputtered, and we rolled into a spot. I popped the hood and waved goodbye, assuring her that spark plug replacement was well within my realm of skill. The first three screwed out easily with the satisfying click of the socket. The fourth was directly beneath a metal bar, so I contorted my arm, burnt the side of my hand, crawled beneath to lie on asphalt hoping for a better angle below. The socket head slipped over the plug, but then there was no room to crank the handle. I made room to gain more leverage but lost hold of the tool, ramming my knuckles into the block. My chin broke the handle's fall. The socket head was stuck tight to the spark plug's head. I decided to take a walk. A gas station must be nearby, and I could use a drink. By the time I made the two-mile hike, I was thirsty once again but had cooled down with the help of walking meditation and a sprinkler system that had gone awry. The second attempt ended as badly as the first. I got inside and cranked the key, hoping three new plugs would do the trick. The engine groaned, then clicked, then caught, but threatened to stall when thrown into reverse. I gunned it hard, heard a loud pop, gunned it again, and heard a sound I was certain an engine should not make.

Had you been inside the hotel lobby and seen me pass through the glass door, you'd have gathered up your children and quickly turned in your room key. I had grease stains on my khakis and both hands were black. A single vein strained on my forehead, threatening to blow. My last thirty-five cents went to leave a message on a friend's answering machine, something along the lines of "Why the hell aren't you ever home?" My calling card was rejected when I tried someone at work, and my request for a ride from a stranger was unapologetically denied.

The upside to "The Curse of October" is that, in an Edward Abbey sort of way, it gets you out of your car, off your horse, and into ditches with the possibility of being snake-bitten, run down and shedding some blood. I was ten miles from work, but the day was nice, and I was mad as hell. I crossed against the light at the off ramp, passed under the overpass, and by a man holding his cardboard sign, who nodded with understanding as I wove through cars stopped at the light; I didn't look homeless in my dress pants and button down, but he knew as well as I no one was going to pick up a guy with a shaved head and unruly moustache. And for the first time of being stranded, I didn't want anyone to stop; I wanted to walk far and fast, burn off this frustration, absorb some of the city I'd tried so hard to escape.

I'd lived in this city for eight of the best years of my life. Gone to college, met my wife, made some great friends, got my first real job. And as I walked, I passed by hotels where we'd had dinners or wedding receptions for close friends, movie theaters and the mall where we'd often go on dates, bars and restaurants, taco stands and gas stations where I'd stopped a hundred times to buy beer on the way to parties in someone's crummy apartment complex. It had once been the magic city, but most of the people have moved away, as have my wife and I; the highway stuck in traffic is my only connection with this place. In every city the same movies are showing, the same beer is on sale, gas prices fluctuate with hotel rates, and the menus and stores are all serving and selling the same thing. My feet pounding on the sidewalk (I never slowed my pace) gave me a strange, renewed conviction that we had been right in trying to escape. It's true: you're still the same dolt no matter where you go. But, if everywhere you go is tending toward uniformity, the attempt to locate new scenery, to separate yourself from the fray, might eventually erode the inner landscape, and give birth to someone with which you can live.

The friend who's never home was home when I got to work. He agreed to pick me up and take me to see Mike the mechanic that night. I called a guy in South Austin, whose shop we had used when we lived in town, and he agreed to take a look at the car. None of the love that had bloomed the previous evening remained when I arrived at Mike the mechanic's. I announced that the car he had safely sent us off in had blown up and stranded me once again, and he announced that the truck I'd had towed in had nothing wrong, but I owed him for labor. We exchanged money and keys and agreed to part ways. I was halfway home when I stopped for gas, but when I was ready to leave, the truck wouldn't turn over, so I went back inside, bought some water, and got change for a one. I called Mike the mechanic, but he was already gone. Darkness settled in, and I sat on my tailgate, drinking water, watching crickets flock to the light of the pumps. Half an hour later, the truck turned over, and I drove home without stopping and without the radio.

The next few days it ran fine until it got hot. I cleaned the battery terminals with Coke and wire-brushed the connections. Planned my trips carefully, never stopping if I couldn't leave it running, never shutting off the engine unless I had half an hour to kill. The price tag to fix the car came to $800; I told the guy in Austin not to bother, but when Christa returned from her conference, she said we had no choice. Getting to work was becoming a board game. Roll the dice. Spin the wheel. Advance three spaces. Go back four. Pick a card. Any card. Sit out one turn. Go to hell. Go directly to hell. Do not pass go. Do not collect $200. Pay every player half of all that you earn. Pinhole leaks kill you slowly, like a crack in a dam.

A boat, though, brings you closer to the things you seek, like the fish that don't need to be reeled in as far, diminishing the chance of losing a bass that like to flip across the surface. And once the fish is out of water, you can merely swing him to the side and into the boat where should he come unhooked, he's trapped safely between the live well and front seat. I've lost a few from shore, at the water's edge, who backflip themselves to safety, a bit shaken but alive. I've followed, on occasion, knee-deep in water, boots sucked in mud. A boat also allows you to move closer to a submerged tree, or a line of tall weeds in water, a splash that could be the big one, or even to the other side of the lake where the water looks calmer, the sun not so hot. It can also cut down on lost lures, since it allows you to troll or row to the spot of the snag where, if need be, you can reach into the water and free the lure by hand. A boat can bring you closer to the physical things you seek, but the intangibles become more important once you have a boat of your own.

THE RISK INVOLVED

The alarm sounded at 6:00 a.m. the first Saturday after I got my new boat. Still asleep, I made my way to the workshop, loaded the trolling motor and fishing gear, returned to the kitchen for coffee, and set out for the lake. Most mornings hold no magic for me; if I wake before the sun, it's not for leisure time to watch it rise; it's to work or travel, and my lids remain heavy until mid-morning or beyond. But for fishing late season, there's a window of time you don't want to miss by sleeping in, especially if you've just bought a boat. I eased the trailer into the water, first try, parked the truck, and stood on the shore. I've seen mist rising from water by moonlight so rarely it can still make me pause, create the illusion I've stepped into another realm, that I'm about to embark on a spiritual journey, even if I'm only going to tool around a lake like an old man, lose lures, and perhaps catch nothing more than perch, scare turtles, and return home mosquito-bitten and hungry.

Submerged trees with the upper branches breaking through the water's surface are a bass fisherman's delight, and so I was drawn to the far side of the lake. I trolled along the ledge in no rush to make a direct route to the group of sparse trees. The first rule of fishing is not to be in a rush to do anything but get to the water. For a while, the only disturbance was my motor's hum, the small wake from the aft, and bullet head weights or pliers I dropped by my feet. An occasional cottonmouth whipped and slid along the smooth surface. I drifted too close to the shoreline and had to use the oar to keep from bumping into docks. Nothing was tugging the line except a few snags. I watched the surface, tried to discern movement, imagine what lay beneath, and will the fish toward me. It works at times. Probably luck, the serendipitous moments when what you wish actually happens, but only because the odds are bound to strike. If you have your line in water long enough and think about fish swimming past your bait often enough, there'll come a time when the thought meets the hook. The prop groaned and the boat shifted abruptly to the left. I'd struck mud, so I flipped the switch to off, grabbed the oar again, pushed away from the shore. My eyes never leaving the spot where the line met the water.

Duck's chatter drew me out of the trance, and to my left, in someone's backyard, thirty or more were resting on the lawn and dock. A large white goose strutting along in their midst. I put the motor on low, nudging the handle with my elbow to keep a straight tack, and began moving toward the duck-filled lawn. A few flittered away, hopped, then committed to flight, squawking after one another across the lawn and lifting from the water's edge. I silenced the motor and let the wind push me slowly along. The familiar behind me—the dam, the dock, my truck—disappeared, and before me sat a small white house that sagged, in need of paint, black tar-paper roof, a cracked and crooked cement back porch, a rotted wooden fence on one side, twisted barbed wire on the other. The dock that spread from their shore was no longer accessible. Six posts stuck out of the water leading to a platform, but the planks for the walkway were gone. A chair bolted to the platform. And yet, it didn't strike me as crumbling decay; it struck me as a comfortable hideaway, where a couple had spent their summers, and now that they were gone, the ducks had taken over.

As I slid within a few feet of the shore, two ducks flapped their wings and took flight with a clatter, and the ones directly behind them followed suit, and the row behind them did the same, and so on, like a feathery ribbon being lifted to the sky. The noise was tremendous and a bit unsettling, and they circled overhead, scolding me for disturbing their morning rest. A few touched back down on shore but took off immediately when they saw that I was still in range. Danger. I could have had a gun and picked off a dozen or so had they remained on their webbed feet. I could have used my fishing pole to wrap around one's wings or feet and pull them from the air. I don't know that ducks have named these things in their minds, but they recognize anything larger than they as predator, and I have, on occasion, sought them out as prey. That morning, nothing was further from my mind, but their memory and instinct, inherent or learned, that caused a few to settle down and take off while more from the air took their place, created a beautiful dance, a flying circle that

THE RISK INVOLVED

dipped down to touch the earth. A performance I caused, took part of, enjoyed. A reason to get away from it all.

I drifted, mesmerized, until the trolling motor struck sand several hundred yards from the shore. The water was clear and once the silt settled, I dropped the anchor and looked for fish. Made lazy arcs with my fishing line toward a set of bare trees marooned in the middle with a white crane perched on top. I caught a thin bass, no more than ten inches, removed the hook, and placed him back in the water. He paused, unsure of what had trespassed, and darted out of sight. A half hour passed, maybe two, and I pulled the anchor. A rush of black silt and water swirled at my feet. I flipped the motor's switch, and it purred then stopped. I used the oar like a cane until I no longer felt bottom. Flipped the switch again, but the battery was dead. A breeze had started up, so I had to row against the current. Three strokes on the left. Three on the right. Pause to rest, catch my breath while I quickly drifted backward. I was exhausted and a bit relieved an hour later when the bow finally scraped the concrete ramp. The exertion of energy, loss of time, didn't matter. Fishing time is not real time. Crack of dawn melds into midmorning. Hours flicker and disappear like sunlight reflected off scales. Afternoons stretch endless into sunset. A good day of fishing always ends long after dark.

The risk involved in getting away from it all is that it becomes increasingly difficult to return. There are places that strike a chord in us, and the thought of not spending time there makes us ache, and so we'll go to absurd extremes to stay. I bought a new lawn and tractor battery for the boat later that week, but the trolling motor ate up the power too fast. Meanwhile, the truck continued to stall, and the wait became longer in between starts. We finally bought a new car for Christa and used the truck only to haul the boat to the lake. I carried wrenches in the front seat to disconnect the truck's battery to use in the boat. I drove Christa's old car to work until it began to jerk and stall again. Late one Friday night we met at the Ford dealership to buy a new truck. Once the paperwork was signed, I drove home to pick up the old truck to trade in. It took me two hours to get back to the dealership. The last time it stalled, I was stopped at a red light at a busy intersection. It was pitch black, and I sat watching the light turn from red to green to yellow back to red while people blared their horns and swerved to pass me on the right. Finally, a policewoman stopped and got some folks to help push me into the ditch. Where you live may not be as important as how (though our mad dash to fill graveyards of automobiles suggests otherwise), but both should be linked to how one's living is made, and I think we become more disconnected the further these two things drift apart. But until I can find a way to bring them together, I'm willing to continue the risk.

My grandfather, Charles, took a boat to work every day; he lived in Kentucky, near the banks of the Ohio River, and worked in a logging plant in Cleves. I imagine the calm, the fog off the river, the steam from a thermos, and the deep satisfaction of pulling the engine's chord every morning, the low rumble and pull across the water's surface, sending bullfrogs croaking into the muck, and white cranes lifting like so many sheets on a line. Even rain doesn't disturb the image. The struggle to stay afloat in the face of high wind and waves. Fear of drowning, if survived, makes one's resolve to stay that way stronger, heightens one's sense, underscores the obvious, but seldom tested, axiom that it's good to be alive. Creates the illusion that it's a state that will forever remain. Even barges hauling hogs and sorghum moving down the Ohio like icebergs, while crisscrossing the currents in a two-man boat doesn't disturb the image. Even crawling from bed an hour earlier to make time to crush a path through thin ice and the pull of a wool collar around the neck to leave the shelter of the tree line and face the spray of near freezing water over the bow. Even the winter when the Ohio froze solid, seventeen feet deep, and every mortal man on both sides could walk on water, even if just walking to work. Nothing disturbs the image. Everything seems worth the risk.

INSATIABLE

Step inside—you've never been here, but it's been too many years since someone has called you *honey* and asked *what'll it be?* Take the table in the corner with your back against the wall, the one covered in vinyl, a forgotten shade of green, with cotton poking through burns from cigarettes. A hub of ketchup bottles (never the brand the label says), and those little pickled peppers no one ever seems to eat, just a dab will do Tabasco, plastic flowers in a vase, and ersatz sugar packets stuck together tight with gum. The best places to eat, if you're eating on the run, is a place that seems like home, like the place where you come from.

Take the menu, fingerprinted with axle grease and paint, a sign that the folks who ate before you only do so when they're hungry, and this is where they eat. A place that understands the four food groups are chicken, sausage, pork, and beef. Order anything deep-fried that comes with gravy, Texas toast, or that's been smoked fourteen hours over pieces of mesquite. Save some time with the side dishes and just order them all—corn on the cob, green beans and pinto, fried okra and coleslaw. Potatoes baked. Potatoes scalloped. Potatoes mashed, and French-fried. Don't forget the salad bar, one free trip with any meal, 'cause they've got croutons, thousand island, shredded cheese, and bacon bits.

THE RISK INVOLVED

The iced tea comes in a quart jar, and the waitress will be by to fill it before the level dips below the letters on the side. No need for sweetener; it's fresh brewed, so you don't have to hide the taste. Take a long pull. Use your sleeve there. No one's watching. No one cares. You've made your order. Tilt your chair back. Watch your head there. Yes, that's real. Farm equipment bought at auctions or perhaps an antique store—scythes, a harness made of leather, rusted rakes and hoes, an ax, hobbles, chains, and buckets, hanging on the wall beside pictures of downtown when the streets were cobblestone. A license plate for every year since 1952 like rusted garland along the ceiling sometimes strung with Christmas lights. Check the chalkboard daily specials for quail and rabbit, if in season, and frog legs while they last. There are restaurants that mass-produce a rural ambience; you'll find three in every city, but please be aware: instant grits, like instant coffee, are never worth the wait.

Parking lots should be considered, from the gravel to the door, if you're in search of biscuits that don't come from a can. No yellow lines or blockades are usually good signs that the folks who run the place are still focused on food. Don't let the waitress out front smoking make you turn to leave; she sincerely likes the fact that this is her second home. Look for pickup trucks, still square, but newer ones will do, just check the bed for bits of hay, specks of oil, and a chain. The salt of the earth go hand-in-hand with blue-collar food.

My wife and I have made it to the country, and though it may sound strange, one drawback of moving here was our choices for eating out dwindled from over a hundred in the city down to exactly five. This is significant because we fell in love over food so many times—starting in college, late at night, when she'd knock at my window, and because I had a car, and because she had some cash, we'd get two-for-ones at the drive-thru, eat our fill in the parking lot; eventually we moved inside to build-your-own burger barns, mixing mayonnaise and chopped onions covered with toasted buns, and then onto places with waitresses where it still didn't matter what we wore, and when I got a part-time job, we had dinner, drinks, desserts, until we had reservations, and I wore a suit and tie, and asked her to get married after a meal of veal and wine.

We got real jobs and apartments, electric bills and car loans, so for a year or two we tried eating at home. She became a vegetarian. I became a fast food freak. We ate rice and beans and noodles. She returned to eating meat. We bought cookbooks and made pancakes, waffles, carrot stew. We burned everything imaginable before returning to our first love. We found the best restaurants were buildings that used to be somebody's home—turn-of-the-century bed and breakfast serving French toast with cream cheese, topped with berries and pecans, edible flowers, and washed down with coffee in china cups, hazelnut and freshly ground; homes turned health food haven, in neighborhoods you'd never find if you hadn't asked directions, if you hadn't seen the sign, where the hostess greets you on the front porch and leads you down the hall to a bedroom that's no smoking with local artwork on the wall, serving red zinger iced tea with nothing that's ever had a face, bread fresh baked in a brick oven, spinach dip and artichokes.

Some days, now, it is necessity, driving home long after dark, to order spinach pizza with onion rings on top; some mornings, it's a ritual—breakfast tacos served with chips; weekends, it's entertainment since we moved to a town without bowling alleys or theaters, miniature golf or shopping malls, so Friday nights we move like hunters, driving down country roads to flush up hidden restaurants and pounce to eat our prey; Saturday afternoons are more relaxed, so we may amble into town for smoked chicken and antiques, some ice cream if it's warm; brunch on Sundays, it's a buffet, fresh salad, omelets, fish, drinking coffee for an hour, listening to a string quartet. We've been married for five years, and our anniversaries surround trips to restaurants or to cities where we've heard the eatin's good.

THE RISK INVOLVED

A restaurant in Seattle that overlooks the Puget Sound serves Alder plank smoked salmon that'll melt right on your tongue. Squid sandwiches in San Diego are worth trying once or twice but best eaten on the beach, watching girls on bikes go by. I still have dreams of Santa Fe, still have dreams of Pueblo pie. Buffalo burgers in Montana leave the palate parched, and blame the craving for wild game on the Absaroka mountain range. It's best in the Midwest to know a friend or two; they seem to keep the topnotch food at home on the range. Peanut butter and banana sandwiches, deep-fried, can still be found in many Memphis diners for hungry pilgrims Graceland-bound. Cincinnati is still the pork capital of the world, and a brown round from Louisville is worth the trip from anywhere. Longfellow's Wayside Inn, where we spent our honeymoon, serves a nine-course meal on weekends that'll make you a patriot of food.

My wife grew up in Southern Louisiana, and it's the only place to go for catfish, crabs, and oysters, etouffee and clams, red beans and rice, shrimp gumbo, jambalaya and boudin. You might flinch the first time a sack of steaming crawfish is spilled onto the table, and you're invited to dig in. Peel the shell, suck the head, the first few go down hard, but grab a beer, some new potatoes, and you'll be cracking claws, twisting bodies, licking fingers with a mouthful of crustaceans, crying out for more.

No matter how far we travel, Tex-Mex always brings us home. Beef enchiladas, quesadillas, pork tamales, sour cream, chile con queso, and tongue tacos, a chalupa made with beans, flautas, chips and corn tortillas, smothered in hot sauce, jalapenos, habaneros, and cilantro, but remember this: never order "south of the border" if the waitresses are white.

The best place to find your favorite meal is probably still at home. Folks didn't eat out much when I was young in my hometown. My family's garden was as large as the house where I now live, and the first time I ate canned vegetables I decided I'd rather starve. Uncles raised hogs, beef, and chicken, made a holiday of slaughter time. Rare occasions might find us eating at the one restaurant in town, but we mainly used the drive-thru connected to its side where my mother worked in high school, and my father would stop by in his '57 Chevy every day for chocolate malts. But there are strangers in the kitchen of the house where I first lived, and I'm washing dishes with my sister peering out the window above the sink, wishing the sun would stop its sinking, so we'd still have time outside; where I'm sitting at the table hiding every kind of bean beneath my plate and stuffed in napkins, begging to be excused; where I'm watching mother fry up rabbit while my father cleans his gun.

It would be easy to want to return to the white house with black roof, sit in the middle of the kitchen, in the middle of the woods, in the middle of a town that's not even on the map, and the folks who live there now would probably let me look around, but a man I knew from Mexico said his childhood home had been turned into a restaurant several years ago. He returned with friends to visit, sat in the corner of his old room at a folding table near the window, drinking beer, singing along with the accordion coming from somewhere in the house. If he closed his eyes and listened, it was like being home again, but it unnerved him when they were open to see the waitress passing by. Kitchen memories (like others) are sometimes best left undisturbed, best left dimly lit with slanted floors, grease-spattered stoves, wobbly chairs and wallpaper, a matching shade of green.

My wife will sometimes make a meatloaf from my mother's recipe or try something new from *Southern Living* made with bourbon and pecans, but we mostly hit the greasy spoons within close radius of our house, or meet after work in the city to chow down at our favorite haunts. We don't agree on everything, but our love for food is one tie that always binds, and we do agree on this: never stop at a chain restaurant unless change is all you've got. Never not eat at a place just because it looks run down. Never send the order back unless the food is cold. Never try something new if you've found your favorite dish. *Eat to live, don't live to eat* is for those who've never found clam chowder served in bread bowls, the best egg rolls in town, burritos big as your face, Italian sausage, chipotle ranch, beer-battered French fries, Jack Daniel's cream pies, or the perfect chicken fried steak.

Grab the waitress. Pass the napkins. We need more coffee—and the check.

FILAMENT

A slice that rivals any new moon in a black October night, that sends old men cursing for cover beneath their carts' awning on the adjacent tee box, that has put motorists' and small pond animals' lives in peril, would be reason enough to quit. A hundred thousand gallons of pesticide and herbicide used to make a Central Texas field as pristine as a New England countryside in spring should be enough to make one wander into the rough in search of less greener pastures. Green fees and cart fees, soft spiked shoes to replace one's cleats, bags of tees and leather, right-handed gloves, a dozen balls every other week, putters to replace ones snapped in haste, oversized drivers to replace last year's "biggest one yet," titanium-filled everything for better balance, smoother swing, greater distance, a crisper ping, would be reason enough to cut the credit card into a thousand tiny pieces. Young men in matching white shirts and khakis who call you sir, meet you in the parking lot to pick up your clubs, and again on the eighteenth hole to clean the mud from your irons that have not produced birdies and eagles, but rather have left behind double bogey divots along every fairway, should be enough to make a man say enough is enough; bring me my rod and reel to comfort me.

THE RISK INVOLVED

Because when the line unwinds from the spool across a pool of water, blue-black and still, with a whine vibrating the thumb, a hum past the ear, and breaks the surface, is dragged down by a lure, silver and green with sharp hooks, that drifts in a see-saw motion unseen but felt in the palm of your hand, how could you call it anything but ritual? A cast across a pond, stock tank, lake, or stream that hooks slightly to the left, driven by the caster's arm, careens dangerously for a sunken tree, stopped short at the tip of an extended branch, by the quick backward flip of the wrist, is enough to make a man wish he could stay in one place forever. Still waters while you wait, with no motion in the trees or a breeze to keep mosquitoes away. Tackle box by your side with top water jigs, spinners and spoons, plastic worms, rattle traps, hooks of every size, and needle-nose pliers, a bobber and weights, and three pocketknives—the choices are endless, but once you find your honey hole, there's only one bait that you'll use, and a black plastic worm on a number ten hook weighted down by a soft bullet head is pulled, left to drift, pulled, left to drift, pulled, left to drift toward the shore. The moment between the anticipation and the strike in the places denied to the eye, cool and dark, but seen in visions, vivid and stark, is the underwater meeting of you on the shore and creatures ancient as time. It is places such as these from which people emerge with stories of how they've seen God.

The five-pound bass is to fishing what the hole-in-one is to golf, but I began neither pastime with either goal in mind. And while I've fished since I was six, I started playing golf only two years ago, first by chance, and then coercion, then I continued for lack of pride. It was a detour from this quest to land the five-pound bass, and a new obsession I'd developed as an apiarist, but mainly it was friendship, mainly it was Ben's fault. Ben and I met at the chemical plant the summer he was heading for college, and I was about to graduate. We aspired to more than the work we did there: painting handrails, safety yellow, chipping and sanding platforms and tanks, hauling drums from the warehouse, standing fire watch, cutting grass and killing weeds with pesticide. Our lives were about to send us different directions, but we both loved to fish, and in the six years that followed, each time he returned to visit family, we'd slip off on Friday afternoons, pick up a twelve-pack in Elgin, sip beer in plastic cups, camp out and fish on my wife's Grandma's farm in Giddings, returning home late Sunday night.

The summer I began keeping bees, Ben was down from Boston, taking a break from law school. We had talked of going fishing or perhaps hanging out in town, but first we had to make a stop, so I could buy an extra super for excess honey in the fall. I had found a place that sold bee supplies in downtown Austin at a pitch-and-putt golf course. Putters for rent and nine irons line a rack on the store's east side behind a counter stocked with score cards, tiny pencils, bags of tees, and a basket full of loose balls, three for a dollar, slightly used. The west side is home to shelves holding hive bodies and shallow supers, some in pieces, yet unpainted, other knocked together ready to go. A shelf over the doorway holds hive staples and inner covers, protected with a thin layer of dust. On the walls behind the front desk is a list, handwritten in black ink, of every golfer on the course who has made a hole-in-one. I paid little mind on my first visit to retired couples and day-campers as they moved around the nine-hole course. By summer's end, I would have joined them, along with friends, so many times that my name would be included on the wall.

The day I took Ben with me he suggested we play nine holes even though neither one of us had ever swung a club. We rented two putters, two nine irons, bought six balls and a bag of tees. Pitch-and-putt is a cross between miniature golf and the real thing; each hole is par three, so you're driving with a nine. The course we played on is tight; holes two, four, and nine are a few feet from a busy street; you hit toward a fast food restaurant when playing three and five, where homeless men sleep off their beer on a grassy hill next to the parking lot. Railroad tracks hug six and seven; eight sends you back to a busy street, so hook or slice you're in trouble—all the same we played twenty-seven holes. We bounced balls off moving cars, dug divots, ignored the eight-stroke rule, lost three balls a piece on the seventh hole water hazard each time we passed through, and then returned the next morning at eight, paid sixteen dollars and played 'til dusk.

The next day, sore-shouldered and sunburned, I bid adieu to Boston-bound Ben, and I thought, to the game of golf. Then one afternoon my friend, Josh, and I were slated to see a movie, but I suggested something outdoors. Josh grew up in the city, loves the lighting in bars, the chatter of buses, A.C., and fast food. He'd never go fishing, and though he'd never played golf, I figured manicured greens would be closer to carpet than the bank of a dam. He agreed and we played Tuesday, then Thursday, and then the following week; he bought gloves, then a golf shirt, then a full set of clubs. He bought spikes, then a golf bag, then a practice green with a spring-loaded cup that shot back your putt to save you from walking or bending your back. We played June, July, August, twice a week, sometimes three, rearranging work schedules, sometimes calling in sick. We bought balls, reconditioned, bottled water by the case, cursed sundown and blisters, and praised God that Texas summers never bring rain. Started bringing home scorecards to prove to our wives we weren't having affairs, just becoming old men.

Then my father-in-law came to visit with a mismatched set of clubs, real woods and iron blades, grips as worn as the bag, rescued from the garage where they'd been awaiting a yard sale. We set out to play on a real eighteen-hole course, a few miles from my house, even though I'd never used a driver or any iron one through eight. The course is cradled in a state park, full of hills, high weeds, pine trees. We didn't rent a cart, but after several holes, I realized only four-wheel drive could have saved my game. I couldn't drive, couldn't chip, couldn't putt, couldn't breathe. Couldn't make par, read a green, judge any distance, choose the right club. Couldn't stop cussing, or complaining, apologizing through my slice, wondering what in God's name I was thinking taking up this game. Somewhere around the thirteenth hole my scorecard and the mercury hit the century mark. I'd lost fourteen balls, broken a dozen tees, contracted poison ivy, and so stumbled to the car. We had only paid for nine holes, so it wasn't a total loss.

I remember losing seven lures within an hour of my first throw on a rainy afternoon with my brother-in-law years ago. On two occasions, the tip of my rod had snapped off mid-cast, and once I set the hook so hard, the pole cracked, bent in two, swayed with the zigzag of the fish's movements to shore. I've lost a pole completely, broken a handle when the reel was cast into the pasture for failing to catch fish. And the line has snapped from sunken tree limbs or pulling a fish too hard. Poorly tied hooks have run away on the lips of stronger fish. I've been mosquito-bitten and sunburned, scared by snakes, stuck in the mud, rained on, almost struck by lightning, and nearly drowned rushing into water to retrieve a five-pound bass that had made it to the shoreline before breaking the line to run.

Fishermen lie; it's a fact, and tales of largemouthed bass hooked between the eyes with a top-water Hula-Popper by a moonlight midnight get left untold, but I'm here to tell you this: a hook driven through my jaw pulled taunt followed by sudden suffocation would not kill the thrill of the strike, the shouts of fish on the line! This is how I know: once I struggled with the three-prong hook wedged deep in the largemouth's head while Ben stood, hook in thumb, long neck bottle between his teeth, blood down the front of his jeans, a catfish in seizure at his feet. The pain and suffering, albeit self-inflicted, caused no empathy for the fish, not because of a dominion over animals clause, but because of something that predates it by a billion years. This: we know the hook is coming, be it cancer, car wreck, or the long slow fade. We're here for the blood and the struggle, and we're here to have some fun.

Fishing trips *can* go bad that way. Poison ivy and snakebites, fire ants, wet socks, heat stroke and rain, dry rot line, broken limbs and lures. The

THE RISK INVOLVED

One That Got Away. Fishing trips can go strange. A primeval surge is not unheard of, and I have photographs to prove it—a pyre of plastic dominoes fueled by bourbon, lit with cigars. Fishing trips can go feral. Rather than traipse around the tank after losing seven lures, I once stripped bare and swam across to my tackle waiting in my truck. Fished until sundown in boxers, boots, and a straw cowboy hat. Fishing trips can take you anywhere the spirit leads.

And you don't need a tee time to fish. You can wear boots, collarless shirts, and flannel. Bring your own beer. Drive on the greens. No marshal to move you along. Game wardens exist, but I've never seen one in the wild. One can fish socially, but solitude is best, something one wouldn't consider while swinging the clubs: a great shot in golf is like the proverbial tree falling in the woods; it loses its effect if no one is around. Fishing trips are like grooves burned into wax; you can play them over and over again in your mind. Fishing is not a single act, but a casting backward. The filament that stretches from where I live now, within walking distance of Indian Lake where I fished just this morning, back through Yellowstone River, Eagle Mountain Lake, Giddings and Brownwood, Texoma, Bear Creek, the Ohio, Whiskey Bay. It arches and loops around people I reach only via e-mail, or see only at weddings, or will never speak to again. It holds thousands of fish, and if you look closely, it glistens with memories encapsulated in beads you can touch, taste, and smell.

Nothing about golf strikes me as natural. I've no sentimental connection, no history, no skill. To do it right, you've got to keep your head down, "keep your eye on the ball" like your little league coach repeatedly told you, or pretend, as a colleague of mine insists, that there's a string tied around your head, the other end around your nuts. If you look up, the game is over. There's little room for error in the game of golf. Left arm straight, right arm crooked, hands loose, end over end with pinkies locked. Break your wrists, not your back. Slow on the back swing. The goal, in golf, is not the hole in one, it's to advance the ball, and to do it right, you've got to make the sweet spot of the club strike the center of the ball. My golf game is good, right up until this crucial point. Everything goes south (or east or west) the moment the club hits the ball. This pendulum swing is akin to the fisherman's cast, or so it seems. The only difference being is one is overhead, the other underneath, and while I've hit tree limbs and shrubs with a pole as often as I've hit ground, broken the tee and sent the ball skirting askew to bounce along the cart path, the difference goes deeper than motion.

The back swing of a club holds the weight of a cinder block. You're pulling the tension of the last four failed drives, along with as many made on this very tee box, coupled with the stares of friends, perhaps a few strangers, who murmur encouragement that's really critical advice in disguise. If there's a foursome waiting, the pressure increases tenfold. There's your feet to consider, too wide spread, not aligned, and your grip that's too tight, too high or too low, and the wind that's too hard or the ball's teed too high; there's a dogleg ahead. Did they say right or left? All of this rolled into a knot in the back of your neck with more tension than the thousand and one rubber bands spun inside the ball.

And then there's the back swing made with fishing pole as gentle as wind whispering through a long willow branch. Adjustments can be made for low hanging branches with a horizontal drawback. The right arm outstretched. Or if placement is vital such as dropping a lure at the edge of tall cattails without causing a snag. An inch forward to lay the line in front of fish you can see near the bank; an inch back if a lazy cascading across open waters is what you desire. Best of all—a clumsy plunk, line tangled around the reel, can also land you fish. Just break the surface with the bait. An average rod weighs eight ounces, but you feel nothing at all as it hangs for a moment like an elongated finger that's been there since birth. The tension that's present is fluid, relaxed, from the tip of the rod to the shoulder's sinews. Twenty plus years of this arm's repetition has provided this comfort; this relaxed backward motion, which is why I must give up on golfing and focus only on fish.

Both fishing and golf are simply hobbies, and one could argue the hobby itself is not important; it's the quality of time spent. When I fish with friends or family, it's a mixture of honing a skill, pure joy and relaxation, but mainly the conversation, catching up or making plans, sharing stories, working through problems or just blowing off steam. The same can be said for golf. The difference is I never fish with strangers, and I never golf alone. Some men will golf with anyone, show up without a tee time to tag along with a threesome whose fourth man overslept. I prefer to golf with guys I know, who don't mind mulligans or waiting while I search for my ball in tall weeds. On occasion, a friend and I have had a pleasant morning golfing with strangers like a couple in their seventies who politely put us to shame or the guy who slipped off the first tee box midway through his back swing. But mostly it's just men, better dressed and more equipped, to whom we spend all our time in apology, and none on our mental game.

The mental game, in anything, is an extension of one's overall mentality; it's how we view who we are. When you'll rise at 5:30 to string elk hair flies in Montana to catch cutthroat trout, or snag largemouth bass in a hundred-degree Texas heat, fire ant bites all down your leg, or even catch perch with corn kernels in creeks near a suburb, and your palms still sweat in all of these places, the first strike of the day kicks you awake more than coffee, and you'll stay there until sunset on the promise of one bite, then you can begin to call any place home. Understand the abstract notion of one's inner peace is not linked to possessions, but lies somewhere between the unseen pull in dark places and a pair of dry socks.

The mental game, in anything, is an extension of how we live. We've played at several courses with fairways lined with homes, and after I got over my fear that I'd break someone's window or brain a small dog, I begin to wonder what kinds of folks live in houses near golf courses. I don't know because I have yet to see anyone in their yard, so it must be people who don't do yardwork or really enjoy the great outdoors. In all fairness, I've never been at one of these courses at night, so the kinds of people who live on golf courses must work regular, long hour jobs in order to afford living where they do. I also can't help but notice, while searching for a lost ball in the rough, that these places are rough because they're in the middle of what once was a forest or somebody's field.

My love affair with golf will be short-lived because my mental game is tied to place. I met a girl in college whose grandmother had a farm forty miles east of Austin, full of stock tanks bursting with catfish, and the beloved largemouth bass. It was there that an obsession grew out of a pastime; I became happiest at sundown with a fish struggling on line. The girl and I got married, and we moved fifteen miles from this place. The stock tanks' measurements itself would not convince you this is my favorite place to fish. Perhaps the cluster of trees, dead and surrounded by water in seclusion at dusk with dusty sundown, a backdrop for cowbirds perched white on branches would, but that doesn't matter; I don't want you here. I'd give you directions from Austin, Bastrop, or Houston, but I'm bad with numbers; my memory is flawed. The size and number, availability, of fish might make you scurry through the phone book searching for the name of my wife's grandmother, but her hearing is shot. She doesn't like strangers. You know fish breaking water's surface far from the shore is the easiest way to lose him, but if you've witnessed this dance on a January dawn (fishing through the winter is quite common here), then you know no fevered revival comes close to the joy, no modern day miracle matches the wonder of *another soul has been won. Hallelujah!* If you know this, then you might come, despite all my warnings, but if you do know, then I suspect you've got a place of your own.

THE RISK INVOLVED

There's more to life than fishing, and there are worse ways to spend an afternoon than playing golf. More to life than fishing and fates much worse than death. The crux, though, for me is faith in something unseen. Hope that the lure you've cast, the spot you've chosen, dime-sized and remote, along with wrist movement, subtle, direct, will land fish on the line, fish at your feet. It's also love of outdoors, competition, and struggle. It's a cathedral of trees without the hard pews. And grace. The standing in place, memorizing sun glint on water, fresh cut hay from a field, mud between toes, so you know you can return here, that *I don't deserve to be here, but I am*. And when it all comes together, you're transcending time with no thoughts of overdue payments or fast-coming deadlines. And if I have hope in life after death, it lies buried somewhere between a mound full of fish heads and kernels of corn, tales of the fisher king restoring rain in the wasteland, and men casting nets to the other side because their good friend could walk on water. I fish because it's worship, and the lure hitting the mark is my prayer that something pure, something good, will come.

SWARM SEASON

Banners rippled at the wind's behest, hovering over crowds that milled and buzzed. A spectrum of color against a backdrop of brown grass, restrained by the sidewalk and a traffic cop's hand, awaiting the signal that would free them to spill over the curb and into the street. I watched from my truck, stopped at a red light. The light changed to green, and I moved down the road past shorthaired women and men in a rainbow array of t-shirts, holding hands, holding signs, holding up traffic with their protest parade. An hour before I stood with my wife, "brushed with the hiss of rustling wings" as our hive threw the first swarm of the season.

Christa was planting Lantana and Indian Hawthorn in a bed she had dug next to the shop. I was burning tree limbs and brush we had cleared for a fence in a pile stacked higher than my head. The center sent off a rush of heat I could hear, but over the crackle and draft, Christa was calling my name. I slipped my leather gloves into my back pocket and walked to where she stood pointing a trowel.

"Hear that?"

"It's the fire."

"No, I think it's the bees."

THE RISK INVOLVED

Our hive sits on the east side of the house about twenty feet from the back door. The house and laundry room block wind on two sides, but it still catches the morning sun. We can also raise the shade in the bedroom and watch the bees as they work while we're lying in bed. As we turned the corner of the house, the hum turned into a buzz. Bees poured from the entrance, dripped down the side, clustering on the cement blocks that hold up the hive, churning on the ledge like dirt from a plow, moving up the side and filling the air. Hundreds formed a funnel taller than the house, sunlight catching their wings as they ascended and spun.

Cold fronts breaking or sunshine after several days of rain can heighten a hive's activity. A hundred or so will rock back and forth near the entrance, making a pattern that mimics thread on a loom, but the flurry of bees was more like a whirlwind as I crept 'round the laundry room to approach the hive from behind. I hoped they had cabin fever and were getting out to stretch the legs, fan the wings. Christa circled the house and stood thirty feet in front of the hive, scanning the four large oaks that grow on that side of the yard. Two are close to the hive, but just over the fence are acres of trees. I hoped they'd choose a limb on our land, one preferably low to the ground.

"There they are," Christa said. Through the veil of bees I could only see her shading her eyes with one hand and pointing with the other to the sun. I made my way through scrubby trees and brush, following the fence line to where she stood.

"There's a clump, baseball size. About thirty feet up."

We watched the mass swell as more bees piled on, and I added my six feet to our six-foot step ladder, envisioning myself balanced precariously from the top rung, adding two more feet for an outstretched arm's reach and still came up over fifteen feet short. Within minutes, the chaos ceased as though the floodgates had been closed. If I could capture the swarm, I could begin a new hive. We live in the country, and the nearest place to buy bee supplies is in downtown Austin at a pitch-and-putt course. The logistics could be solved on the two-hour drive, so I grabbed my keys and the checkbook and left Christa on the phone soliciting advice from folks more seasoned in the safe handling of bees.

The old man who runs the course washes golf balls on a stool by the window, and sometimes he's sleeping in the sun. He's eighty, maybe ninety, only hears what he wants to, doesn't recognize me even though I stop by once a month. After slipping through the parade, I made my way to the clubhouse, shuffled my feet, faked a cough, and rattled the old man awake with my keys. He placed a nine iron and putter on the glass counter, but I said, "I'm here about bees." The equipment sits on the other side of the shop, and I could easily gather whatever I need in the time it would take for him to fold the paper, take off his glasses, and slide off his seat. But I waited patiently as he handed me a brood box, ten frames of wax-coated foundation, bottom board, inner cover, and telescoping top. He paused between frames to answer the phone and wait on the men who'd come there to golf. I stacked what he'd gathered until the counter was covered, causing the duffers to pause to double check signs to make certain they had the right place.

The old man figured the prices in a small spiral notebook. He read me the total, and I handed him the check.

"My first swarm of the season," I said, gathering equipment.

"Where'd they land?"

"In an oak tree, about thirty feet up."

He laughed. The first time I'd seen him express any emotion other than anger or boredom.

"I've heard of guys shootin' the base of the limb to knock down a branch."

"That's a thought." I've been dove hunting a dozen times in my life and only been able to knock two birds out of the sky. The shotgun approach could mean a bee massacre.

"They think it's spring already. Mild winter, no freeze. Mine have been going crazy for weeks."

"Good weather for golf."

THE RISK INVOLVED

"I guess."

He put my check in the drawer and returned to his chair as though weather good for anything hadn't concerned him for some time.

The return trip to Smithville landed me in the middle of the parade, and while I waited for the policeman to weave traffic through the crowds, I listened to the vibration of people and the hum of idling cars. The energy that only a city can provide is one I thrived on in my twenties, but one I crave less and less. The constant flow of cars and faces, sitting behind a city bus, exhaust and mindless chatter, waiting in line for everything. A healthy hive of bees can support sixty-thousand bodies in a space the size of a filing cabinet full of dividers, drawers, and paperwork. It shouldn't surprise anyone who has lived in crowded quarters that after only two months of gathering nectar and service to the queen, the average worker bee is ready to drop dead.

The cop waved me into a U-turn that sent me five miles out of my way, past apartments where I lived for too many years, one with friends and three with my wife. The liquor store where I'd drive through on most afternoons on my way home from the chemical plant. Theories abound surrounding bees' swarming behavior—weather, overcrowding, weak queens, but I like to think they grow restless, sick and tired of the same ole grind, living in quarters with thousands of siblings. The wear and tear life of the working bee. My theory, of course, doesn't hold. Swarms aren't rebelling against anything, evidenced by the fact that they take along the queen where they find a hollow log or an attic to continue the only business they know.

I finally pulled into our drive and crushed the emergency brake. The stepladder sat with an open jar of honey on top beneath the branch that just hours before had been garlanded with bees. Workers will stay at the swarm site, usually overnight, protecting the queen until the scouts return with a detailed report, delivered in dance, regarding directions to a new hive location. The branch, though, was bare. I scanned other branches, stepped back to glance over other trees, moved toward the fence line, but saw nothing but bark lichen and leaves.

"They left about an hour after you did," Christa said from the porch.

I wanted to scream, throw large objects, try the shotgun approach on an empty limb.

"I walked through the woods but never saw which direction they went."

"It's not your fault."

I needed a beer and a walk through the woods.

I covered just over two acres, stopping beside every tree, knocking on ones that looked hollow, peering into holes on tiptoe. Considered driving through the neighborhood, looking for an exterminator's truck since a garage or front porch eave will often strike homeless bees as a good place to begin again. It seldom strikes the owner that way. My walk yielded no bees, but the opportunity to meander through the trees always makes it easier to breathe.

They're insects and we have thousands. I've a full-time job and don't need the honey to sell, don't even care for the taste, but sometimes enjoy chewing the comb. The most common mistake a beginning beekeeper can make is too much manipulation of the hive when bees do best left alone. The swarm had cheated me out of a reason to handle them up close once again. It was early spring—still time for the hive to build to sixty thousand, to pack more pollen and honey than we could eat, sell, or give away. But I don't keep bees for the numbers. I keep them because few others my age do, for the murmur they make when I open the hive; for the elbow-deep-in-bees sensation I get even while wearing long, leather gloves; and for the thrill of watching them spiral with sunlight reflected on wings. I keep them because they never pay heed to the idea that they are creatures that need to be kept.

Two weeks later on Easter Sunday, everyone was here—Christa's parents, aunts and uncles, cousins and grandma. A few friends on their way. The women cooked potatoes, made Jell-O salad and dessert. The men wandered around the yard, made small talk, drinking beer. Smoked pork tenderloin was the main course, and my only task was to man the grill, so I started drinking Shiner as soon as we got home from church. The coals were hot and I'd hit that zone where a week of preparation was over. The guests were here. Time to relax.

"I think the bees are swarming again," Christa announced from the front porch.

A whirlwind of bees can excite fascination if you've never seen one before, but two swarms in as many weeks, is enough to kill a peaceful buzz. The family had gathered at a safe distance admiring the rush of bees by the time I rounded the corner, slipped behind the laundry room, followed the fence line, whacking shrubs, to meet Christa beneath a tree. The swarm was headed in the same direction, but this time had chosen a new tree, one that grew next to the house, one without any low limbs. A clump was forming on a branch about level with the roof. The men followed close behind, looking relieved that there was something to do, so I called out a list of things we needed while waving them toward the shed. One uncle hefted the ladder. I handed another uncle the tree saw, removed a few frames from an empty brood box while Cousin Stan gathered pieces of rope. Christa's mom stopped me at the shed door and said the fire was going out. I wedged the box beneath Stan's free arm because I knew there was no way they'd wait.

One uncle was halfway up the tree by the time I'd soaked more briquettes. The saw didn't even reach from the ladder, so Stan was tying a rock to the end of the rope. Everyone was still clustered near the base of the tree. I wondered what kind of disasters my homeowner's insurance covers, as I envisioned the rock smashing into the center of the swarm, Christa's uncle falling over backward, and the family covered in bees. Stan flung the rock which made a perfect arc over the targeted branch and landed unattached. The rope fluttered at his feet.

I ran back to the grill, struck a new match, and flames engulfed the meat, so I slammed down the lid, waited a few seconds, flipped it open again to a pouring black smoke. The meat might taste a bit charred and a little like fluid, but I wanted it to hurry. I wanted everyone inside. Christa's uncle had the rope over by the time I returned. The men alternated taking tugs on the branch, but instead of a shower of bees and a holiday ruined, nothing much happened at all. A few rose from the clump each time the branch moved but then settled down once the motion stopped. The brood box sat empty. The bees all sat tight. The women lost interest and returned to the house.

Christa's mother emerged half an hour later to announce that dinner was served. I had forgotten the meat and wondered about my friend, Carlton, but decided I was hungry so wrote off the swarm. The prayer freshly finished, Carlton knocked on the door, asked about the ladder, was filled in on the swarm, shown to his seat, and entertained us with stories. Carlton has a B.A. in philosophy, religion, and biology, a Ph.D. in genetics and evolutionary biology, a photographic memory, and more books under his belt than anyone I've met; he also got me interested in bees. The meat was then passed, a bit smoky but tender, beans wrapped in bacon, potatoes, and salad, the glasses re-filled, seconds offered, declined, the bread remembered and used to sop up the plates, coffee made, pies cut and served, thanksgiving returned, and we hit the door.

How we ended up on the roof I don't quite remember; there was more wine with dinner, but that's no excuse. After Carlton had his turn tugging the branch, he suggested we get a frame full of brood from the hive. I showed Stan how to start the smoker and had him cranking on the bellows. Carlton gathered twigs for fuel while Christa's uncle remained with the bees, pulling on the branch. I got suited up and we descended on the hive, pulled a frame from the bottom box, and shook off the bees, cut a hole through the corner, threaded it with rope. I handed it to Christa's uncle who ran it up the tree. The idea was that the bees would cluster around the brood, and after we had lured a large number, we could lower the frame into the new hive.

THE RISK INVOLVED

A bee suit will make you sweat in almost any kind of weather. That morning it rained off and on early, so it was humid, and I was drenched. I grabbed a beer and went to change while everyone remained watching and waiting for the bees to make their move. I don't know how long we waited, but I pulled up a lawn chair, and someone began to tug the rope since the bees were ignoring the brood.

"We've messed with them long enough," I finally announced.

"What if we tried brushing them onto the frame?"

"It's too humid. They might be cranky."

"You think a broom would work?"

"They're too high. Forget it."

All I can say is we're guys. The slightest presence of danger means that we'll never give up. I scrounged up a brush-looking pole used to knock down cobwebs and dirt. Stan duct taped PVC pipe to the handle, and we handed it off to Christa's uncle who hadn't left his post. The pipe was too flimsy and the brush waved in the air, occasionally hitting the bees.

Someone mentioned trying from the roof, and I went inside to change shoes. I was wearing cowboy boots and didn't think they'd fare well on a roof made of tin. The ladder was set up on the porch by the time I made it back outside. Stan was handing the brush to someone whom I quickly surmised to be Stan. I joined him and we crawled up the slope, balanced our way across the apex. We stood watching one another, our feet uncertain.

"A package of bees costs only thirty dollars. I'm certain you're both worth much more," Carlton offered from the front yard. He'll be the first to admit when it comes to rolling up your sleeves for some one-on-one with nature, he'd rather read about it in a book or analyze it in the lab.

Stan took a few swats at the bees, but his arms were too short, so I took the pipe, just long enough to reach the swarm, and gently began brushing the bees onto the frame.

"It's working."

"Easy."

"Rolling bees might make them mad."

"Shit. Shit. Shit."

I heard a sound like a firecracker that spins when it's lit just before a bee popped me beneath my left eye. The brush hit the ground, and I heard Carlton shouting, but by the time I turned, another bee drove her stinger above my right eye.

"I'd get down if I were you," I said walking slowly toward Stan who sat like a statue on the peak of the roof.

"I'm kind of afraid to move."

"Just move slowly. You'll be all right."

"Get the stinger out," Carlton called from the ground. "Brush it gently with your finger so you don't release more venom."

I've read and heard contradictory information on the importance of removing the barb once you're stung. The sac on the end of the stinger continues to pulsate once the bee falls away. Some say the longer it remains, the more protein spreads through your system. Others say if you're allergic, once the point is in, the damage is done. I was stung a few weeks before, the first time since I was young. I was in a rush to put a new brood box on and a cranky bee nailed my lower jaw. The side of my face and neck swelled a bit as the evening wore on, but I hadn't thought to look for the stinger since I had a week's worth of stubble at the time. I shaved later that night, and after I did the final wash, I was amazed to find that the stinger had survived a double blade. My face was normal the next morning, so I decided I wasn't allergic to bees.

Nonetheless, Stan brushed the two stingers from my face, and we made our way down the ladder. My body temperature was rising, but I wrote it off to frustration, humidity, and beer. The looks of the family when I lit on the porch suggested that perhaps I was wrong.

"You're starting to swell already."

"Looks like they were going for your eyes."

"Does it hurt?"

THE RISK INVOLVED

"Thank God you didn't fall."

"You should have quit."

I wondered if anyone had heard my suggestion we quit before we climbed onto the roof. The stings had swelled to half-dollar size by the time I got to a mirror. Christa rubbed cream and gave me two antihistamines, but I read the side of the box and the alcohol warning and decided to only take one. The conversation ceased when I returned to the porch and everyone checked out my head. Everyone except Christa's uncle who had picked up the brush and continued to prod at the bees. My hands began to tingle and my stomach to itch. When anyone spoke to me they focused on my head. I announced, "I'm going to change clothes."

My entire stomach and mid-section were covered in a rash, and by the time I changed, I had hives—on my hands, up my arms, inside my armpits, down my legs, on the tops of my feet. Christa met me in the hallway, and I showed her my arms. She got her purse as I put on shoes. Carlton came into the kitchen.

"I've been thinking, maybe you should go to the hospital."

I showed him my arms as I walked to the door.

"We're on our way."

The hospital is only five miles away, and the waiting area was empty. My blood pressure was checked while Christa filled out some forms, and they asked if I had trouble swallowing. I had been taking small gulps since we got in the car to make sure my throat wasn't swelling shut. My head, though, must have looked quite impressive because once I was led through a curtain and sat on a table, everyone on duty just happened to stop by. I was given two large pills and a small cup of water.

"I've had a few beers, is that going to hurt?"

"Nah, these will take down the swelling," the guy who handed me the pills said.

I popped them in my mouth.

"You chewin' them?"

"He's afraid of choking," Christa chimed in.

"Christ, are you having trouble breathing?"

"No, a horse pill got stuck in my throat when I was a kid. I always chew pills."

"Oh, I wish you'd have told me. We've got that stuff in liquid."

After about five minutes or so, a gentleman in a white lab coat walked over, poised with a shot.

"Looks like you've been sunbathing."

I looked at my shorts and flip flops.

"No, I was just hot after I got stung."

"No, the rash on your skin. Looks like you've been sunbathing."

I was certainly glad to provide entertainment on a slow Easter Sunday afternoon.

He swabbed my left arm, and I looked away. The least painful of the three injections I'd received that day. A new warmth spread through my body as Christa and I waited and talked. We decided, all things considered, the food had been delicious, her mother's decorations nice as usual, the conversation not too strained. That getting stung on the head was unconventional, but an effective way, nonetheless, to clear one's house in a hurry of holiday guests.

Christa gave updates on my face every ten minutes, and by the end of the hour, the swelling abated, and the hives disappeared. The doctor returned, told me to be careful, and take antihistamines every two hours and then sent us home. Everyone was gone except for Christa's parents. The swarm was still in the tree, but I didn't care. I lay on the couch in my office reading Notes of a Native Son until the beer, shot, and pills overwhelmed me and knocked me clean out.

My left eye was swollen shut when I awoke the next morning. It was still dark in the house, but I found my way to the bathroom, and even without glasses, peering through one eye, I knew I was a mess. I went back to bed. A few hours later Christa woke me up. Her parents were leaving, but I declined the offer to tell them goodbye. After they left, I put on my glasses, but my cheeks were so swollen, the frames sat lopsided on my face. I returned to the mirror for a closer inspection. The flesh around both eyes protruded an inch farther than normal. The left eye was still shut. My entire face was round. I wouldn't have recognized myself had I seen my face in a picture. Christa was sympathetic and polite, and by mid-afternoon we had a good laugh. She said the swarm was gone, and we wished them good riddance. I lay in bed reading the whole day, popping antihistamines every two hours, and by bedtime that night the swelling had gone down. I called in sick the next morning because my left eye had swelled shut again. The bridge of my nose was almost back to normal, and the following day I was still a bit puffy but went back to work. I suffered a few chipmunk jokes and holiday weight gain cracks, but I guess you've got it coming if you're going to keep bees.

They're insects and we have thousands, and I decided to keep them after reading four books. Everything I'd read said bees aren't aggressive in a swarm. They've got no brood or honey to protect, so they're not likely to sting. I'd seen pictures and heard stories of beekeepers in t-shirts and shorts removing swarms from branches without so much as a veil. Of course, I'd also read that most beekeepers will write off a swarm if it's so high you need a ladder or if conditions seem unsafe. The idea that they're creatures of a predictable nature never occurs to the bees, which is why I'll climb rooftops to knock them from trees.

The phone rang on a Thursday morning, the first week of summer. I'm an errant member of a beekeeper's association, and during a meeting I missed, Carlton put my name on a swarm list. An older couple in South Austin had a swarm in their yard, and their niece was calling around to have them removed. My previous attempts and lack of brood boxes, the fact that they lived an hour away, and the restless nature of bees who had sat two days in the rain and would likely rise up now that the sun had broken through, didn't stop me from asking directions. I wanted to capture a swarm.

"One more thing," the lady said before I hung up the phone, "my uncle wanted to make it clear that he's not charging anything to pick up the bees, but he's not paying anyone either."

"Understood. If all goes well, they'll be rid of the bees, and I'll have enough to start a new hive."

I called the number the niece gave me, and her aunt answered the phone.

"Where exactly are they?"

"Just sitting on the ground."

"And they've been there two days?"

"They landed in a pecan tree, and yesterday started to fly around, but then it started raining, and they just fell into a pile in the backyard."

"Is it raining now?"

"No."

"I'll be there in a little over an hour."

"There's one more thing. My husband wanted to make it clear…"

"I don't have to pay you, and you're not going to pay me. Got it."

Two weeks before, two full brood boxes and four shallow supers had arrived in the mail, and I'd spent several evenings banging tiny nails into thin wood, sliding wax foundation into the creases, tacking on frame spacers, and painting the outside of the hives. After the paint had dried, I split the active hive into two colonies with the hope of preventing any more swarms. This left me with only shallow supers, and in order to capture a swarm, I really needed a full-depth brood box. I'd read of swarms being captured in bags or makeshift boxes, and since I didn't have much time, I decided to bang something together.

I pulled on a pair of jeans after hanging up the phone, grabbed a long-sleeved white cotton shirt, stuck a box of matches in my pocket, and ran to the workshop. There are stray pieces of wood lying all along the back wall, and I picked up a piece that looked like it would completely cover a shallow super. I made a rough cut with my saber saw and nailed the wood to the bottom of the super, then grabbed my bee suit, smoker, staple gun, an old piece of window screen, filled a coffee can with

THE RISK INVOLVED

charcoal and covered it with fluid, scooped up sawdust shavings with another empty can, threw everything into the cab of the truck, and hit the road.

The old man and his neighbor were waiting in the drive to greet me as soon as I stepped out of the truck. They knew a bit about bees but wanted to know why they had landed on the ground, why they'd swarmed in the first place, and what I was going to do. An image of my swollen head crept into my mind with each question I answered, but I had driven for an hour, so I fought off the urge to pretend I had the wrong house and crawl back to my truck.

The old man pointed toward two pecan trees in his backyard.

"Keep walking straight ahead. They're right between 'em."

"Let's take a look."

"Is it safe for us to stand here and watch?"

"I'm not going to do anything yet. You can come along if you want."

"Did my wife mention that I'm not charging you for the bees?"

"And you're not paying me either."

"Right."

"It's a fair deal. I've never actually captured a swarm."

I walked briskly toward the pile to avoid any more questions.

They looked like a glorious, writhing mud puddle. Since none were flying, I bent over for a closer look. The easiest way would be to find the queen, put her in the box, and wait for the rest to follow, but I've never been able to pick out a queen in a mess of her workers.

I walked back to the truck and began suiting up. White coveralls, bee veil, and gloves. I left the smoker for the moment since I was already taking this extra precaution. Halfway back to the swarm, the old man asked if he could take my picture.

"You don't have to pose. I want an action shot."

I rested on my haunches, running my fingers through the bees, hoping his idea of action was a smooth transfer of bees from the ground to the box. A hum rose as I made a few passes through the swarm. There was no way I was going to find the queen. I looked up just as the camera snapped. I poured a handful of bees into the box. To my surprise, most stayed, so I repeated the process until there were more bees in the air and in the box than were left on the ground. I stood to let things calm down, and saw the two men kicked back in lawn chairs, each one drinking a beer.

"You want one? We also got wine, whiskey, and moonshine."

"I might have a beer when I'm done."

"Is it working?"

"I think so. I'm going to get the smoker started to see if I can get them to stay in the super."

The lighter fluid I soaked the charcoal with before leaving the house must have evaporated because match after match landed in the smoker, burned a few seconds, then gave up the ghost. I looked for twigs lying around, but the rain had left everything damp. My glovebox was full of receipts, check stubs, and napkins, so I grabbed a handful of trash and began stuffing lit paper into the smoker.

"You got any lighter fluid?" the neighbor asked his friend.

"How about alcohol? That burns, doesn't it?"

"You mean rubbing alcohol?"

"Yeah. I got an electric grill."

"It burns, but not for long."

"I got gasoline."

I was fanning the paper, pumping the bellows, and praying something would catch. I appreciated the men's eagerness and desire to see flames leaping from my smoker, but I could see yet another attempt to capture a swarm taking a wrong turn. The old man emerged from the house with a bottle full of clear liquid. I thought he was kidding when he offered me moonshine, but indeed it appeared the man had some on hand.

"This shit will burn."

He dug the cork out with his pocketknife while I furiously lit matches, blowing on deposit slips that smoked and glowed but never caught on.

THE RISK INVOLVED

The old man leaned over and poured moonshine into the smoker. A white-hot flame flared for a second, then nothing. Some paper was smoldering, so I stuffed the smoker full of sawdust and began pumping hard. I didn't think it would last long but wanted to return to the bees before the old man disappeared into the garage to seek gasoline.

Two separate clumps had formed in the box, a third dripped down the side. I couldn't tell which held the queen, so I smoked them all in an effort to make them unite. A handful was still on the ground, so I scooped them into the box until almost every bee was either inside or hovering nearby. I moved the box about ten feet away and returned to check the original spot. A large bee, looking rather royal, was crawling along the ground with a few attendants in tow. Frustrated that the queen wasn't in the box but relieved that I now knew where she was, I scooped her up gently so as not to crush her with my leather gloves, placed her in the super, and stapled the screen over the top. Covered in sweat and eager to shed the bee suit, I practically skipped back to my truck.

"God damn, we did it," the old man said, handing me a beer.

"I finally rustled a swarm."

"You get all of 'em?"

"Enough."

"What becomes of the ones left behind?"

"They'll die."

"Right away?"

"A day or two, I suppose."

"Nothing for 'em to do, I suspect," the neighbor sighed.

We sat in lawn chairs, and in the midst of a whirlwind of questions about my wife, my job, politics, and religion, three beers and few bees that had been left behind, a revelation occurred: I keep bees because they're creatures one could buy and sell, but in order to work them, they have to roam free. I keep them because pesticides and parasites have virtually made the feral bee disappear. I keep them because once folks know that you do, they always will ask you, "how are the bees?"

JEFFREY UTZINGER

And this: my grandfather kept bees, a man I never met, but about whom my father tells stories of walking on comb, licking honey from his hands; and my mother's father did about whom my grandmother said, came home one afternoon after helping his brother coax swarms from hollow logs, stung seventeen times on his arms and his head, which swelled so badly that by nightfall he looked like a stranger lying in bed; and the stories old men tell at beekeeping meetings—the average age, sixty-five—and they all bring their wives, and notebooks with dates, written in pencil of the day every year the white clover has bloomed; and the stories Carlton tells of a boyhood in Indiana, two hives his parents bought him that grew to fourteen, and lifting a cover on a day it was raining, having his t-shirt pinned to his back, or sitting with binoculars on sunny afternoons watching workers land with orange and red pellets tucked in their legs. I keep bees because I long to be that little boy, discovering fear and a fascination for life, and because I want to live long to become that old man with half-moons of wax beneath fingernails, propolis stains on white cotton shirts, dispensing wisdom, sweet as honey, from a tattered notebook.

FORTY DAYS OF THIS

She washes her face, dabs it dry with a towel as I watch over her shoulder, attempting to shave, both of us watching the image of how each appears to themselves, the opposite of how we appear to the world, and though she's beautiful there in the mirror, she applies a light base, rubs blush on the cheek bone, the thick black mascara to lashes, a subtle eye shadow that makes me realize I wasn't aware she wore any at all, and though I'm transfixed by her face, I stop to rinse the razor as she steps out of the way, and I miss what I love the most, the pursed lips ready to receive the red waxy lipstick, catching only the tissue floating to the waste basket—a kiss suspended and falling, and then gone. I look up to see that she's smiling over my shoulder, our images reversed, and I turn to kiss, reversing the image again, and as she puts her hands to my face to rub the smooth skin, I touch my lips to the tip of her mask.

We're unusually close, sharing this space in the mirror; we've been together long enough that we're more likely to seek our own time in the morning, but we're out of our element, staying at her brother and his wife's apartment in New Orleans. We arrived in the city to rows of young black girls bearing down, kicking spandex legs high, adorned in silver sequins, ruffled skirts and bright bows, their leader twirling a baton. We joined the parade *in medias res*. Stepped into the street on the heels of the glitter girl's last swagger and dance. Trombones and the cymbal crash of the marching band swelled, the final note of "Iko, Iko," *talkin' bout Hey now (hey now)* blended into an unfamiliar tune, with a hint of a Latin beat. I stood in the middle of a blacktop street so narrow cars would have to drive half in the ditch to pass, beneath a canopy of oak tree branches. A tractor with goal posts mounted to the front, painted yellow and blue, rolled lazily by, not at all a threat to the twirling, cheering squad, but enough to keep the parents and sponsors and a few exhausted girls with their pom poms hanging at their sides who were lagging behind, moving at a reasonable pace.

I've moved at a reasonable pace through the preceding nights and days. It's been two, maybe three; I've lost track of time. Late nights. Early mornings. Heavy sleep with no dreams. We did our own dance on Friday in Austin, kicking drawers shut, holding paperwork at bay, and spinning out the door early to drive like mad for the Mardi Gras. Christa grew up in Baton Rouge, and this celebration along the Mississippi, fit for such a wild, muddy river, is nothing new for her. I've never been, however, and at first, I didn't want to come. I'm loath to spend a weekend away from the country where we live in a small town, on an acre of land, surrounded by trees near the Colorado River. During the week we drive two hours round trip each day to work in the city, so the thought of driving for hours to relax, smacked of madness, along with the sleeping in guest beds, eating what others choose, spending all waking hours talking with people. Travel brings out the beast who usually sleeps, and he's prone to lash out. It gets ugly.

I'd also expected scorching heat, projectile vomit, crushing crowds, and overwhelming fatigue, but my first glimpse of a parade was two blocks from a university that we passed after parking along a residential street lined with hundred-year-old mansions that looked brand new with immaculate lawns and gladiolas in bloom. I hadn't expected to get close enough to the floats to reach out and touch the rider's hands, and in many ways, my first glimpse reminded me of a small town parade. And soon after we arrived, Christa spotted her brother and squeezed my hand, laughed, and pulled me from the path of the yellow and blue tractor, forward to the curb into the shade among spectators yelling and waving their arms. My sister-in-law strung beads over our heads, and her husband handed me a beer. Her family was lounging in a grassy median beneath trees, waving for us to join them like we all lived in the neighborhood and had just walked from our house.

I had expected chaos but found it natural to blend into the crowd, to fall into easy conversation with strangers while men in ludicrous rubber masks or with scarves across their mouths hurled throws, plastic cups, and doubloons. I hung back that first afternoon, believing the trinkets were for children, but each time a float passed, the adults rushed forward, waving their arms, so I inched forward and caught my first strand, lightweight and green. It circled around two fingers and I felt a lightness, an understanding, almost a relief. My brother-in-law handed me another beer as I slipped the beads around Christa's neck. A plastic cup hit me in the back of the head, and I felt better than I'd felt in some time.

I didn't know, the first afternoon, how addictive all of this would become, didn't know I'd want the span of time to stretch on for forty days or more, but began to understand when six or seven floats had passed, and suddenly, the first parade was over, and I felt the child-like disappointment. We'd arrived too late for this one, but it was only the first of many parades we'd join. And though nobody spoke of plans or emerged from the crowd as a leader, we began to move as one; at first, I thought toward the parade's mid-point, so we could revisit the marching bands' tunes or heckle the float-riders with "hey mister," but it was more like movement on a raft in a river, being carried toward an uncertain destination, lulled by the sounds and the sway. A movement I slipped into with ease at that moment and have followed for the duration of our stay.

We came to rest on the steps of an enormous white stucco apartment with a narrow stairwell, lined with a cold iron rail that spiraled to the top.

THE RISK INVOLVED

It smelled of mildew but the people ascending and descending, drinks in hand and laughing, made the atmosphere crackle, the hallway sparkle and shine. I don't remember who lived there, or even if the one I'm remembering was the first we visited that day—our sister-in-law has friends and family spread all over the city.

The houses and apartments we have visited are all tiny, but we've gladly squeezed inside. A double bed with several lounging people usually sits near the door. Mimosas and fried turkey are crammed on narrow kitchen counters. Love seats pushed next to tables on which sit plates of ham, potato salad, crab dip, and tortilla chips threatening to push small TVs over the edge. A narrow hallway usually leads to other rooms full of more people, more alcohol, more food. An ever-present line for the bathroom whose end is never sure circles the room, but I can fall into conversation with someone at some point and eventually be granted a turn. At one stop a man told me there was beer in the bathtub, so I waited in line, used the facilities, and grabbed a beer. When I emerged, the guy said *you'd better get two*. And I did. Dionysus has moved through the day into darkness, handing me bottle after beer after bourbon, making me think I can drink like a young man again. And I have.

Tonight we leave for our final parade with the moon so high and full following over our shoulders through the black silhouette of tree branches and street signs as we walk through neighborhoods that rose up beautiful and white. Christa's hand is as warm in mine as I imagine the hot burning stars to be resting in the folds of the sky so clear and midnight blue. The bourbon and water that has replaced my blood reminds me I'm so much in love, makes me fall back on the sentimental phrase, makes me skip and talk too loud. We cross railroad tracks, and our group reconvenes to merge in the crowds lining the streets to catch a glimpse of another parade.

We catch the parade in preparation, still and churning as though it's been dammed. The source of the stream that will wind its way through the Big Easy, carrying lights and masked men on ornate floats made of flowers, plastic and *papier-mâché* Herculean forms, smiling gypsies, mermaids. The men aboard talk, swill beer from silver cans, pulling handfuls of beads—purple, yellow, and green—from boxes and bags they discard in the street, a casual preparation for a full night of work. We move, our pool of relatives and friends through this sea of people; we've arrived too late, lingered too long over cocktails and light conversation, the kind that moves through a day so relaxed you haven't noticed the time, the kind possible only when strangers are mingled with family, and nothing of import needs to be sorted. Too late to really carve out the perfect spot on the curb.

A family friend who's a lawyer and collector of cowboy boots, a man who always wears slacks and a sports jacket, pulls cigars from his coat and begins passing them around. I draw the flame in as the smoke fills my mouth. My wife wanders off with her sister-in-laws' parents, back to view the static floats. I watch as they admire, then grow closer, waving to the men in masks. Christa pulls the band from her hair, shakes her long blonde ponytail loose, and waves to the men on the top tier. A swirl of large green beads move heavenward and swing down around her outstretched arm. Her movements and laughter, rare revelations of her coy nature, the flirtation with strangers, moves me to the year we met and I began falling asleep at nights with her image in my head.

I look back down the alley of the static parade, swarms of people milling in conversation, clinging to keep warm, and the colored lights that have begun to flicker on floats, on street posts, and from glow-in-the-dark charms, children are swinging on strings. The first float begins to move. An enormous cheer erupts. I find Christa and we move back to the group. The crowds are like tides swelling, our hands shooting upward like flecks of foam, lashing out at nothing really—plastic beads, Frisbees, and trinkets.

It makes sense to reach out the first afternoon, when the first float passes by and you stand there naked waiting to be adorned; you want the beads to show you belong here, you're a part of this swell, but midway through if it's too hot, and you've had too much beer, and bodies are pressing too close, enough to drown you, it doesn't make sense to roll your arms like a drowning man—it's not lifesavers we're grasping; it's more weight. And midway through your stay, your second or third parade, if beads hang like mill stone around your neck that has turned bright pink from where sweat bled a cheap set into your skin, and hundreds, already procured, lie in a tangled seaweed glut on the backseat, strung around the rearview, draped across the chair and under the bed, or a boxful sits in someone's apartment, removed to ease the burden and forgotten in a peaceful stupor walking home, then it seems ludicrous to cry out for more. But when the float passes by and there's a lull, the void seems insufferable. The crowd recedes to catch its breath, the road and curbs like the beach at low tide littered with beads that miraculously sifted through hands and touched down. Nearly no one stoops to pick up these treasures. There's something magical about snatching it mid-air. It's a tradition that comes from Spain, but its actions seem so American. The thrill of the wide receiver. The hunger for more of the same.

This annual apocalyptic celebration—one more sin before the beginning of Lent— somehow seems out of order to me. Forty days of abstinence, and self-denial should be followed by forty days of this.

This masquerade seems more of a chance, for an evening, to forget your failures and fears. It's a chance to move through an evening without anyone questioning whether the visage you wear is real, or if you're only holding a mask. It's an evening of levity, weightless illusion, surrounded by beauty with no time constraints. It's a chance for the things, real or imagined, that separate a family to evaporate in brisk coastal air. And if it's just an excuse to eat and drink more, work less for a few days, then well, that seems okay too. Religious ritual and pagan rites aside, it's easy to get lost in a parade.

And this one is winding down. The wind feels a bit more brisk, our steps slowed and speech sparse. As the crowd disperses, a discussion ensues about where we should eat, and though I'm suddenly overcome with hunger, I think I'd rather curl up next to Christa and sleep. We cross the street to where a line of men in orange jumpsuits with white plastic bags slung over their shoulders have emerged from the shadows. A man with a whistle barks a command, and the line of convicts move in methodical unison down the sidewalk, picking up trash. Every detail perfectly planned.

A siren blares, and as we step out of the street, a paddy wagon big as a city bus bears down, red and blue flashing lights on top, and bright neon lights inside, lighting the faces of those who stepped out of line, faces more weary than afraid at the prospect of a night in jail. My brother-in-law yells *go deep*, and I trot back into the street, my feet feeling for the curb, my eyes over my shoulder. He rears back, lets the plush football fly. I lose it in a streetlight, catching instead a glimpse of a beautiful woman who's become haloed in the street cleaner's spray. A boy intercepts the pass and runs off. I stand and watch, amazed at the stranger she's become. At the beauty of water and refracted false light. Bells from a fool's cap jingle, and for a moment, I pretend we are saved.

WOODS WALKING

North Bend Road starts in downtown Hebron, Kentucky, and slopes by a church with a towering steeple where my parents were married and I was baptized; the road runs east past the bank where the good name of my parents could still secure a loan, crests a hill where trees replace streetlights, and passes a horse farm owned by my father's friend; it winds through the houses of people's names I've forgotten, pauses beside a white house with black shutters where I lived for the first ten years of my life, and drops off a steep hill with tight curves (white-tailed deer clinging to its shoulders) and dense forest, picking up speed before disappearing into the Ohio River valley lined with tobacco fields, cattle, and old men on tractors cutting hay.

I'd like to believe that my hometown still exists as perfect as it stands in my mind. That the white house with black shutters is still surrounded by trees, as it was twenty years ago, and a wagon wheel still leans on the trunk of a Chinese elm whose branches spread over the house. A house left to my father the year both his adoptive parents died. The same year my mother and father got married, tore down the outhouse, installed indoor plumbing, added a new living room, and made the old place their home. Where my first memory is housed at my father's feet, listening

THE RISK INVOLVED

to Hank Williams on a scratched vinyl record. Where the kitchen floor slants toward a long room in the back with a washing machine and a sink. Where we played with beagle and blue tick puppies on the cold cement floor until they were big enough for the kennel outdoors. Where we played badminton, croquet, hide-and-seek, and kick the can, waiting at dusk for the lightning bug flash. Where we built snowmen, flew kites, crashed bikes, and rode sleds down an enormous hill behind the house that led to a valley and a forest that stretched on for miles.

The house sat alone on five acres, but I thought we owned the world.

There's another house on the opposite end of North Bend Road; it's also white but has two stories, a basement, and a massive front porch. My mom was a girl there in a black and white age. I'd like to believe I could still step off the back porch and walk through bee-covered clover, past a white-washed, cinder-block barn where my cousins and I built hay forts and rode a mattress, hell for leather, down the steps and out the barn door, ran through fields of Black-Eyed Susan, taking cover in abandoned chicken coops, raced through rows of alfalfa and corn stalks and into the woods to shimmy up birch and maple trees, collect leaves and shiny, dark buckeyes, resting on the forest floor that smelled of water and moss, removing our shoes to wade through the stream, searching for arrowheads before climbing up a hill to a clearing of cattle onto my uncle's dairy farm and sliding, finally, down the dam toward a pond to fish for bluegill, sunfish, and perch.

My paths to these woods were suddenly cut off the year I turned ten, the same year the state built a highway through the middle of my grandparents' fields, separating their land from my uncle's, which was also the same year my father's company transferred us nine hundred miles down the road. I imagined Texas was a land with no trees, a place where it never rained, full of tumbleweeds and cactuses, scorpions, and rattlesnakes. What it held was much worse. We arrived late July to a house and scorched lawn, the entirety of which would have fit in the vegetable garden we left behind in Kentucky. We lived subdivided for the first time with a single pear tree, no taller than me, in a backyard surrounded with a privacy fence. There was, however, a small field and a few head of cattle right behind our street. I walked home from school that first fall to find my father with a crowbar, ripping wooden planks from the back fence. Each section he removed revealed a strand of barbed wire. I thought it strange but didn't ask what he was doing, simply sat down my books and began to stack planks. I fully understand now, what was beginning only to dawn on me then, as we sat and watched cows graze until dusk.

We returned to Kentucky as often as we could for Christmas, long summer breaks and special occasions until, gradually, our lives took shallow root in Texas and lapses between visits increased. In my mid-twenties, after an absence of five years, we returned for a family reunion. Aunts and female cousins descended the first morning of our trip to whisk away my mother, sister, and wife to go antiquing, which left my father and me with the thing we both found most awkward: time alone together with nothing to watch on television. He suggested we visit old friends and family. Maybe take a walk in the woods.

Cemeteries seemed an odd place to begin, but many of the people my father knew as a boy were dead. We started in the graveyard of a small Baptist church a few miles from the Ohio River. We found names on stone that reminded my father of hunting trips, legendary rhubarb pie, and long family feuds. Like Uncle Harold who took Aunt Sarah to visit her family every Sunday night, but since Harold knew he wasn't welcome, he waited alone for hours in the car. And Uncle Valentine who stopped beneath a tree along his favorite walkway in the woods and was found dead with his hound dog asleep at his feet. And the man who owned the only filling station in town where my father worked as a boy. They went hunting together one afternoon as they had many times, but my father forgot to bring shotgun shells. Even though he never lived it down, it was that day my father realized he didn't care to hunt; he was just most at ease without a roof overhead.

From these rolling hills beneath evergreens, we crossed the bridge to Ohio, where we stood by the graves of my father's adoptive parents. I did the math—both were in their mid-fifties, my father's age now. *I thought they were old when they died* is what I was thinking, and as we walked to the car, my father said it aloud. These grandparents I never met, adopted my father when he was four. After tuberculosis sent his biological mother to bed for the last time, she and her husband, a cross-country truck driver, made plans to divide their six young children among a few close friends. These siblings grew up in Hebron, attended the same schools during the day, but lived with different families at night. Their mother was twenty-nine when she died, and while I have seen pictures of this thin, smiling woman, I know little about her. My father's memories of her are either too faint to recall or too painful to tell.

Back in Kentucky we visited the cemetery behind the church with the towering steeple where my father's mother is buried. Someday, my parents will be laid to rest there as well. My father joked he picked their grave plot because it overlooks left field where he played softball on the church team for years. We wove our way past stones blotched with green and gray moss, running our fingers over names as my father continued to unwind stories about great uncles and aunts, cousins, friends of the family. It was the most I had ever heard him talk in a single afternoon.

My mother's father, who died when I was six, is buried there as well. He lives in my memory as one of the happiest men I have known, almost always in the kitchen in a cloud of flour surrounded by the aroma of rye bread and crazy cake, laughing, making jokes I didn't always understand. At the piano, singing hymns or banging out ragtime songs. My most vivid memory of him is walking behind him in the forest; he stops suddenly, plucks a paw paw from a tree, peels it with a pocketknife and eats it whole, juice running down his fingers and chin. I didn't learn until later in life that this grandfather, as a teenager, left town to travel west, wrote his mother beautiful letters from the road about his inability to find his place in the world. I don't know what brought him home, but he became a jack-of-all-trades because he loved day drinking whiskey and couldn't keep a steady job.

    Too much time with the dead can make you morose, so my father and I left cemeteries and drove down North Bend Road toward the white house with black shutters. The new owners had painted the house a bluish gray and cut down the Arbor Day pine my sister planted in the third grade. The wagon wheel was gone. It is not unheard of to knock on a stranger's door, introduce yourself, explain that you once lived here, and ask to look around. However, this is not something my father (or I, for that matter) would do. It wasn't the house either of us wanted to walk through, anyway; it was the woods behind the house. We sat at the end of the gravel drive for several minutes, and a twenty-year-old memory returned: we're in a 1965 Chevy Impala in this exact spot, and we're both wearing knit caps, and my hands are pressed to the heater vents while my father fiddles with the radio dial, looking for a college basketball game. On cold, clear nights, the radio reception was best in his car, and while he did this often, it was the first time I joined him. It was also the night we both probably realized if I could figure out basketball, we could solve my mother's frequent suggestion that we spend more time together.

    We decided to drive to the river before heading back to town, and as we pulled out of the driveway, another memory came back: a man on a tractor being followed by at least fifteen dogs—blue ticks, beagles, bloodhounds, and mutts—creeping up North Bend Road and stopping by our house. It was an old family friend, Georgie, a man who left his property so seldom his dogs were confused. They barked so loudly and leapt, nipping his face and hands as he talked to my father on the front lawn, I was unsure how the two men could even hear one another. Georgie left his plow in our yard, so he could take the dogs back home.

    A few miles down the road, we pulled into one of the new subdivisions that were cropping up throughout the forests and fields. We parked in a cul-de-sac next to palettes stacked with brick, and my father pointed to a house in the distance that belonged to Georgie, dead now for several years. Since none of the new houses were occupied, we decided to trespass and take a walk through the remaining wooded area, following the faint trail that used to be a long driveway. After quite a hike, we found the old place; weeds were so high around the house, we decided not to risk pulling away any boards that covered the windows and doors. I had been there several times as a boy, but back then you couldn't see the house from any road. Georgie raised blue tick puppies in his kitchen, kept the newborns in a box next to the stove. His house was full of newspapers, rags, assorted tools, junk mail, boxes, bottles, and machinery parts. I stood amazed the first time I entered, torn between the excitement of choosing a puppy and the wonder of a man who seemed to do whatever he wanted, whenever he wanted, and who kept everything that might come in handy at some other time.

We walked around the back of the house and watched smoke pour over treetops from a power plant located across the Ohio River. My father remembered a time flood waters were so high that most of the roads were covered, and he and his father paddled a boat to check on Georgie and his dogs. They used trees along the way as a guide. He told of another time he and his father were crossing the river in a small boat in heavy fog. My father's task was to watch for barges, still in half sleep but shivering, drifting off with the rocking of the boat. *I wasn't worried. Who could miss a barge on the river, even in the fog?* Of course, he did miss the barge, and for a moment, he thought his father's voice was water, so sudden and simultaneous did his father's shout swell with the waves from the barge's wake and slam into his sleepy head. The fear of failing his father shook him more than death by drowning, but the boat dipped backward, settled down, rocked hard, but still afloat. The barge passed by, seemingly near enough to touch, but they sat silent, a foot of water swirling around their feet. I could envision the boat but not the people inside. The space that separates us, my present and his past, seems to span an immeasurable gulf.

I asked about another house I remembered hidden in the woods: an enormous structure, rough-cut like something the earth had uncovered, something as much a part of the land as a large stone. My father lived with several foster parents before he was adopted, and the house was one of many where he had spent some time. We have pictures of great uncles and cousins standing in front of the house, smiling and laughing, holding between them a string of dead foxes on a pole. My father and I walked several miles to find the old house, but our path was blocked by a fence and a gate held tight with rusted chain. The chances were slim of anyone caring if we slipped under the fence, but my father said his back was acting up, and he didn't want to crawl. I also suspected we were moving closer to memories that he would just as soon leave unearthed.

We got back in the car, lost in our own thoughts, and drove back to town to visit the last house on our list—my mother's childhood home. We drove by the white two-story with the enormous front porch but didn't linger long because strangers now live in the house my grandfather built. The front lawn was unkempt, and the house was peeling and chipped, but the most troubling sight lay to the east, across the field where corn used to grow—a nineteen-acre factory rising from the ground. It sits on land where my great-grandparents' house once stood, along with chicken coops, barns, and bee hives. An apple orchard was cut down to lay the parking lot. The family sold the land to a retail dealer who made it the site of their largest manufacturing plant. The plant brought jobs to the area, and a town that isn't growing is dying. Still, with every tree and acre of land traded away, we've given up something I don't think it's possible to reclaim. And there's this: I've worn the brand of blue jeans the factory produces since I was in eighth grade. My remaining connection to the land seems to be denim with brass rivets.

The woods on the other side of the highway are all that's really left of family land, so my father parked his car on the gravel shoulder, and we stepped into the trees. We found foxholes, quail feathers, deer scat, and acorns. Metal from an airplane that crashed here when my parents were young. Beech trees and paw paw, oak saplings thick as weeds; I studied bark and leaf curve as my father pointed to each. We rested at the base of a gargantuan beech, a log chain buried deep in a branch, and my father said when he was younger he could talk to the animals, though he knew the idea sounded strange. I laughed, thought he was kidding, but he rocked back on his haunches, lit a cigarette, and held out his hand, as though to coax something forward from the dead leaves. He said he sat for over an hour late one evening until a fox he'd been tracking came out of a strand of fallen trees. My father stayed still and quiet and began talking to the fox, not aloud with words, but with silent thoughts. The fox would inch closer, and my father would tell it to come, reassuring the animal that he didn't have a gun. He held out his hand slowly, so the fox could see this was true, and gradually the fox drew close enough to touch his nose to my father's pant leg. My father touched my sleeve, and said, *it was just as gentle as that.*

I wanted to ask if he tried to pet the fox, if the fear of sharp teeth prevented him, but that would be my fear. I realized the reason he probably didn't was the same reason I didn't ask: there are moments in life we recognize as rare, and we fear that any movement might disturb the spell. I had been drawn in like the fox by my father's thoughts and didn't want my voice to chase them away, but he stood suddenly, snubbed his cigarette, and said that we'd better move on. The spell broken, I asked what happened to the fox. He laughed and said, *I would imagine that he's dead by now.* Not at all what I meant, but our conversations are often strained, and our meanings somewhat confused. You can't make up the loss of conversations in one afternoon of woods walking, but perhaps it's a place to begin. And as we drove away, I thought of the grief my father conceals or has perhaps overcome. He doesn't drive distracted, doesn't talk much, but smokes, focused on the road. He's been deeper in the woods than I, and sometimes still seems to be.

JEFFREY UTZINGER

❦ ❦ ❦

I was in college before I knew that my paternal grandfather was still alive. After his first wife died and his children moved to other homes, this man tried to stay in contact with his children and grandchildren. My mother said he sent birthday cards and stopped by the house several times when I was small, but my father insisted the only man who had been a father to him was dead. To underscore the point, my father named me after his adoptive father.

I understand you didn't know I was alive is only one of two phrases I can recall that this suddenly still alive grandfather said to me. We met him at his house in Ohio; he'd been just across the river all these years. His wife served us cookies and soft drinks, and we made small talk, but I couldn't get over his easy confidence, how much and how quickly he talked, so unlike my father and me. However, if you saw the three of us together, you'd know by our eyes and crooked smiles that we were fathers and sons.

The second thing I recall my paternal grandfather saying was: *can you believe I gave life to all these people?* It was about a year later when we traveled to his eightieth birthday party. He introduced himself to me several times that evening, which seemed odd, but we didn't know Alzheimer's was creeping in. When he died, my mother sent me his obituary, where we all learned that the woman we met in Ohio was not his second wife, but his third. And this: between his three wives, my paternal grandfather fathered eighteen children.

During our walk through the woods, my father and I came upon two oaks: one of the trees was lightning split, and the blackened half was wedged in the crook of the nearby tree, and I thought how unhelpful the idea of tracing one's family tree is for most people. Families don't have a clear starting point; they don't tell a linear story or follow predictable patterns. Families are more like dense forests, tangled at the roots, tangled at the branches. They separate, fall apart, send out shoots, and grow in unexpected places.

THE RISK INVOLVED

Late in the afternoon, my father and I visited the only grandparent I've known well—my maternal grandmother, who had recently moved to a condo not far from the two-story, white house where she had raised four children. The only thing about her new living space that I recognized from the old house was the 1940s silver toaster with its cloth-covered cord and immense plug. I thought we'd find her dying of a broken heart, given over finally to a longing to see her dead husband in white coveralls, spattered in paint, arms wide with a whiskey-soft grin singing *The Gray Speckled Mare.* That her eyes would well up when she spoke of the nineteen-acre factory, that her spirit would be broken, that she'd be frustrated by the darkness falling over her eyes. I thought she'd be dying of grief, but she's dying of eighty-six years of being alive. She seldom mentions her dead husband, the Great Depression, or life without electricity; she'd rather discuss her children, the weather, or marvel at what her thirteen grandchildren have become. Macular Degeneration is taking her sight, but she never mentions missing the piano, crossword puzzles, or hand-stitching quilts; she's content listening to baseball on the radio and sermons on Sundays. The condo is fine, better than fine; less rooms to clean and no more messing with stairs to get to bed every night.

A painting that hung over my grandparents' couch now hangs in the room where I write. A red wooden barn fills most of the space, but your eyes are immediately drawn to one end that is bathed in sunlight. As you move down the length of the barn, however, the paint grows increasingly darker due to the shade of an enormous tree whose branches completely cover the top of the painting. In front of the barn, a young boy holds a horse's reins while a man re-shoes a back hoof. Beneath the tree, two older men sit on a stone bench in perpetual conversation. And, in the painting's background, there are several white houses, a church with a tall steeple, and a swatch of fields that stretch into a line of dense trees. We were not horse people, but if you were to ask me what my childhood was like, I would point you to the painting and say, *it was like that. Exactly.*

Progress demands growth, builds fences, erects steel, pours concrete, and changes everything you know, but in all fairness to progress, it drove my wife and I to the country when rent prices in the city escalated. First, we moved to the small town forty miles east of Austin and rented a house down a secluded, two-lane gravel road where we lived for several years. The yellow house looked inviting when we'd return home 'round about dusk to be greeted by flowers casting short shadows from lamp light through windows, forgotten in the pre-dawn rushing to work. Since we had lived in apartments in the city for eight years, we realized a new definition of darkness. Gone were the neon tire store and florescent fast food signs. The switchboard effect of apartment porch lights. The headlights, the stoplights, the bright lights of cities that seldom sleep.

We lived on a road that branched off a highway and wound through a handful of houses, twisted mesquite and pine, past clearings for cattle, before it hit a dead end at the Colorado River and fields with neat rows of pecan trees. A month after we moved there, we adopted a short mutt from the pound where he'd landed after eating twelve baby chicks. He was house-bound most of the day because our little yard didn't have a fence. Even though very few cars passed by our house, it was one of those roads that's never patrolled, so the only speed deterrent was soft shoulders and potholes, and no one seemed opposed (myself included) to bouncing down the road at full speed. Christa and I took long walks with the dog most evenings, and people would slow, roll down their window, and ask if we needed a ride. Most folks in the country exercise for a living and don't need to set aside extra time to enjoy fresh air.

THE RISK INVOLVED

One evening, I decided to take the dog to a state park about five miles from the house. I went afterhours, so we could slip past the honor box. We followed the well-trimmed and trodden pathways and color-coded signs for a while before I unhooked his leash and let him run crazy through the pine trees. We came over a steep hill and nearly ran into a deer. The three of us stood stock-still wondering what the other would do. I thought of my father and wanted the deer to stay, wanted to coax her with my thoughts, wanted her breath on my sleeve. I don't know that the dog had ever seen a deer but was certain the deer had definitely seen dogs, and she confirmed my suspicion when the dog let out a howl. White flash—and the deer disappeared. The dog bolted. I followed and we ran with abandon over fallen trees, down and up empty gullies and through ferns, not caring we'd never catch a deer, just giddy to be on a chase. We followed the scent just far enough to get ourselves good and lost. I had a compass key chain, so I pulled it out and looked for the sun. Snapped the dog on the leash and followed the needle in the direction I believed we had come. When we made a broad circle and wound up in the same spot, I unhooked the leash again to let the dog lead. The sun had nearly set before we found the truck again. But since the most danger in my life is driving during rush hour, and each day unfolds as predictable as the one before, it felt good, for a while, to be lost in the woods, following the instincts of a dog.

A part of me keeps rolling around the idea of quitting my job, returning to that white house with black shutters, the half-acre garden, the weeping willow trees, and honeysuckle, and starting a farm, rising before daybreak to milk cows, feed chickens and hogs, spending mid-morning on a plow, taking cat-naps in the afternoon, running to town for tractor parts, with evenings putting up hay, and after supper pouring over bills, wondering why I'd clung to this way of life, but taking one last walk to the barn and seeing stalks of corn against a moonlit sky looking like offerings to the gods, and knowing work is worship, and sacrifice is divine. Or this: I could disappear farther back into the trees and build a cabin in the woods. Chop firewood on summer mornings, fish all afternoon, write into the evenings, and drink myself to sleep. Spend winter tracking wild footprints through the snow. Experience resurrection come springtime, marking off a thousand trails, memorizing every tree and plant that grows within a hundred miles. Keep walking through the woods until I finally make it home.

YOU'RE GOING TO HELL FOR THIS

I stood over an open fire late this afternoon, using a soft bristle brush to sweep bees off honeycomb. Bees I hived from a mail-order package and combined with a swarm I caught; bees I nurtured, fed, kept disease and mite free; bees whose hives I split when they became overcrowded and moved when they became too aggressive; bees I sang to with light smoke and seduced with slow movement—all this to brush them into a fire. A fire I built with my own hands. This might sound like madness. *Bees in the Hands of an Angry Keeper.* A bee holocaust. You might call for my resignation from the beekeeper's association. And you might be right in so doing.

There's no good way to tell this. A better way, I'm certain, of going about this. A voice in my head that insists—you're going to hell for this.

At a meeting years ago, an elderly gentleman told me, "There's a difference between a beekeeper and someone who just has bees." I don't listen well. Drifted off before I heard the crucial part of his wisdom or heard it and have forgotten. I have been determined to be a keeper, but as I watched bees scurry atop a frame of foundation I'd flung into the fire, with bodies curling on contact, falling to a fiery death, and then flames melting through the center, bubbling wax, creating an inferno from which none could escape, I was forced to admit I am one who just had bees. And then I burned them. Quite a change from last spring when I'd successfully captured my first swarm and felt certain I was on my way to becoming a full-fledged keeper.

I had lured a rain-soaked swarm into a super, liberated them from a man's lawn in Austin where they'd sat in a three-day heap. Used a window screen as a canopy stapled to the sides and wedged them into my truck bed between cinderblocks. Kept my eyes on the rearview during the fifty-mile trek home and parked in the side yard to avoid the afternoon sun. Earlier in Austin, I'd drunk beer with the man and his neighbor, and since I hadn't eaten all day, I was feeling a light-headed happiness I knew could take a bad turn, but first I made a batch of ersatz nectar to appease the starving bees. They spread to the sides as I drizzled the liquid from the spoon but quickly rose to the screen when they realized this rain was sweet. Light dabbing motions with a paintbrush works best when feeding bees, but all my brushes had been used to stain wooden floors and chairs. A keeper avoids exposing his bees to toxic residue. A keeper also keeps his bees from open flame.

Some keepers swear by sugar-water solution when late Texas summers bring shriveled blooms, and winter keeps bees confined to the hive. Others use this false nectar to mimic early spring, to kick the insects in gear so they'll produce more honey once the sun encourages flowers to unfold and spores to explode. Still others insist a new hive needs the sugar to stave off starvation and draw out wax foundation. A few keepers, mainly old men—whose disregard for mothering is evidenced by their leathery skin—scoff at the notion of "feeding your bees." Fifty years of healthy hives and high yields seem to be on their side.

I found that I liked the ritual. The two plastic cupfuls of sugar mixed with hot water from the tap. The whirlwind of stirring with a long wooden spoon until the milky solution becomes a translucent swirl. The green plastic pitcher that sits, ever-present at sink-side with a crystallized rim. At first, I boiled water to ensure complete homogenization but learned excessive heat could cause caramelization. A hazardous combination for bees to ingest. I then simply added hot water and let the mixture sit overnight. A thin residue remains like home brew yeast on the bottom, but a keeper develops a steady hand and pours from the top into feeders that come in a variety of styles. Mine are half-gallon glass jars with perforated tin lids. A constellation of holes lightly punched with framing nails so the sugar-water can escape in tiny liquid pearls. Each jar is inverted into the mouth of a wallet-size, wooden contraption that fits neatly into the entrance of the hive. Bees can enter the structure without exposure to predators or foul weather and then cling upside down to the lid while sucking the sweet drops. On warm days they consume an entire half-gallon jar.

The mixture for the swarm was hastily made, but they wasted no time unfurling their tongues to take the sticky syrup from the screen, reminding me that I was near starved myself. Back in the kitchen, I scarfed a peanut butter sandwich, crammed in potato chips, washed it all down with grape Kool-Aid, and returned to the truck to find a smattering of bees hovering over the bed. I crept to the side, detected no rents in the screen, and so decided the diving bees were from my original hive. They had helped themselves to the liquid lunch I'd provided, and the wild loops on the screen were gone. Leaving food for the hungry is not part of the honeybee code.

One buzzed my ear, bumped my chin, perhaps on a peanut butter trail, so I slowly backed away and grabbed the green pitcher. I planned to introduce the two colonies soon, and any keeper will tell you a full bee, sluggish and docile, is easier to work. Gluttony has its advantages. The famished inside hung like a colony of bats, and bees on both sides of the screen scattered as I emptied the pitcher, knocking some down, completely covering others—probably not the best method, but bees are fastidious, if nothing else—their neighbors would clean and preen them dry. Free lunch on a friend.

THE RISK INVOLVED

I'd have suited up in white coveralls, zipped the mesh veil to the collar, snapped the elastic cuffs of the pant legs over the tops of my work boots and the ends of the sleeves over my elbow-length leather gloves. A snug uniform with no inlets for bees, no room for disaster. But that safety suit was returned to a man in town who lent it to me for a couple of years. Now I have a veil with a drawstring neck and cheap leather gloves with elastic that's shot. I wear cotton shirts, long-sleeved and white, that I button to the neck and tuck into my jeans. Normally this is enough, but this morning when I set out to burn the bees, I knew no amount of singing or smoke would soothe them. I pulled a heavy hooded sweatshirt over the veil, my jeans over a pair of sweat pants. Wrapped a roll of duct tape around the jeans' cuffs, the ends of the gloves, my waist where the sweatshirt bottom ended, and my neck to seal the mesh to my shirt. A keeper maintains a level of trust when working his bees; one who merely has bees prepares for the worst.

Swarm day, though, when my hopes were still high, I grabbed my hive tool from the shed and the sports section from the Sunday news, pumped the bellows once more, and pulled the incarcerated bees from the truck. Best-case scenario would have been to house them in a new hive, but I was lacking a brood box, bottom board, and cover. Second best was remodeling, so I carried the shallow super to the existing hive that sat near our back door, twenty feet from a small building that serves as a laundry room. A halo of workers swirled around my head, part welcoming party, part protesting mob. I sat the newcomers a few feet behind the hive, retrieved the smoker from the truck, and returned, puffing cool smoke. A few whiffs in the entrance, a few more in the air. I used the hive tool—a miniature crowbar with razor-sharp edges—to slowly break the seal of the telescoping top. Bees loathe a space without any purpose, so they'll seal gaps and cracks with a yellow, glue-like substance they produce called propolis. Once the top was removed, I lightly smoked the exposed workers in the upper brood box. The effect is my favorite sound bees make—the ones smoked first murmur and buzz like a ribbon being whipped by the wind, and this echoes down the hive, diminishing to a low hum until they're smoked again, and the reverberation repeats.

Quite a change from this afternoon when I cracked open the hives that had been sealed for over six months. The January sky was overcast, and the temperature hovered in the low fifties—not the best weather to work bees. Like humans, foul weather finds them in foul moods. The hive tool dug into the soft wood of the inner cover, and I had to twist the blade to break the propolis seal with a sonorous snap. Keepers refer to this as "the crack"—the vibrations that incite bees to anger—the sounds that keepers avoid. A rough opening jogs their genetic memories, and they crouch ready to pelt bears who have come to offer certain death and honey loss. A one pitch rapid roaring buzz was immediate when I lifted the lid. I stepped back, pumped the smoker's bellows hard, and sent repeated blasts of hot smoke into the front entrance. Placed the smoker's tip over the top edge to blow gusts along the sides of the frames.

Panic is a bee's first reaction to smoke, and some keepers claim bees think a fire's broke out, so they gorge to save the honey that in turn makes them slothful and easier to work. I like to think it's a bit of eat, drink, and be merry, or an insect version of fiddling while Rome burns. Smoke probably just disorients and dulls, evidenced by its crippling effect on their production. Even necessary light doses can slow them for up to a day. Excessive fumes can suffocate, and this afternoon I chose to go for comatose. Perhaps the desire to deliver death without pain.

I've found that I like the ritual of the smoker. At first, I'd stuff the fire pot with dry leaves, collect and snap twigs to make mini pyres in the bottom, drop a match and pump the bellows. Too much oxygen will extinguish the flame, but I became adept at regulating the flow. The flame was perfect when a quick jolt of the bellows sent a ring of flash fire whipping around the mouth. Once the fuel began to smolder and a bright glow appeared, I'd stuff the pot full of dry leaves, clamp down the lid and shoot cool white smoke out the nozzle. Quite a change from

THE RISK INVOLVED

what I've discovered recently—charcoal briquettes doused in lighter fluid will burn fast and long, and sawdust stuffed tight will give off constant, sure smoke. The charcoal can burn too hot, as it did this afternoon as I smoked the hive. Bits of burnt sawdust and flame leapt from the nozzle. And I cranked and cranked until I, along with the bees, paused momentarily, stunned from the smoke.

That sunshiny day in June, the light puffs were just enough to send those lingering on the porch and along the top frames back inside. I placed a double ply sheet of newspaper over the top, removed the staples and screen with channel locks, and turned the super upside down over the newspaper, careful not to crush the bees who were spilling out. I then pried off the super's temporary bottom that had now become the top of the hive. The telescoping cover back in place, I left the rest of the work to the bees. They're highly cooperative, social creatures within a hive but rather xenophobic when it comes to outsiders. If you've ever been stung, especially on the face, you know they can be ruthless. If you've seen those anti-nature *When Insects Go Bad* TV shows, then you think you know they've got killer instincts, but bees nailing humans is really the least interesting aspect of their behavior. In apiaries, the strongest hives often rob honey from the weaker ones. No one simply sits back and welcomes the neighbors; they fight back as best they can. Bees are as vicious as the most territorial animals, and if an unlucky worker lands on the wrong ledge by mistake, she'll quickly be pounced on by several guard bees and knocked from the ledge. However, if bees work together on a project, such as chewing through newspaper (one group on the bottom, the other on top), there's a pretty good chance when they make it through several days later, they're familiar with one another, and the two groups will peacefully merge.

The collaboration isn't a total working-together-makes-everything-rosy ordeal, though. The matter of two queens must be resolved. In rare cases, an aging monarch will be tolerated to lounge while the heir to the throne lays eggs, but the predominant rule is one queen per hive.

When two groups are combined, the queens make their way toward one another and duel to the death. The strongest one usually wins, and so subsequent offspring will be genetically stronger. Anthropomorphism is tempting when studying the natural world, but if you're willing to sit still, observe behavior for an hour or so, trace patterns over a week, month, or year, you might be more disturbed than enlightened. Being busy as a bee can take you far, but sacrificing everything to ensure only the superior survive is a less than admirable quality. Unless you're a keeper and you really want honey.

Reasons for keeping bees are numerous—the most obvious is to steal the fruits of their labor. The relationship is duplicitous from the start, at least on the keeper's part. Rationalization, since L.L. Langstroth's discovery of the "bee space" and creation of the movable frame hive, has been that the keeper can provide conditions that make it possible for bees to produce more honey than they can use in a season. Rationalization too, from the time people first dipped their hands in a hollow log and licked their fingers, simply has been, that honey tastes good. An equally compelling reason in the modern world is that pesticide, Tracheal and Varroa mites, beetles, and various disease have virtually wiped out the feral bee. One could argue that keepers of carefully regulated and well-treated hives have ensured the existence of the honeybee species. Keepers who send their workers to a fiery death, excluded, of course.

Bees have much to offer the natural world, the marketplace, the keeper himself. Pollination of aspiring plants, fields of crops, vegetable gardens, flowers of every kind, shrubs and trees. The strategically placed sting has been purported to ease arthritic pain, pollen to ward off a myriad of ills, local honey to prevent allergies. Royal jelly, honey, and pollen can be found in a thousand-and-one food and beauty products. I've even chewed propolis gum. I wanted to keep bees for the intangibles, though—the pleasure of voyeurism without TV sitcoms, rituals without the trappings of religion, the novelty attractions without theme parks, and of course, for the stories to tell. A good thing these were my original

THE RISK INVOLVED

intentions since in the three years I've kept bees, not a drop of excess honey has been produced.

If patience is a virtue one wants to develop, one may have the stuff of which keepers are made. Year one, after I'd successfully hived my first mail-order package, I had little to do but sit back and wait. The real work of a hive's first few weeks is near impossible to observe. Inside, workers were converting sugar into wax, drawing out the eight-inch by ten-inch frames of double-sided foundation that hold three thousand individual cells per side. Constantly masticating to make each cell large enough to store either honey or brood. Producing royal jelly to feed the insatiable queen who, in warm weather, lays an average of one thousand eggs per day. All I could do was refill the feeder and watch as scavengers returned from the field with bright pellets tucked in their hind legs, making breakneck approaches, skidding to haphazard stops, often flipping ass over teakettle or rear-ending a body that had landed seconds before, then stumbling inside to unload.

They grew that first year from a few thousand toward the hoped-for potential of sixty thousand plus. I tried to estimate the number of workers by counting how many landed on the ledge in a fifteen minute span, but I'd always become distracted by the nudging of legs and rubbing of antennae, the misjudgments in landing that sent a bee reeling over the edge, the struggle to ascend the tall weeds back to the hive. I'd become a rapt audience member to the intricate dance a scout does for other bees. I'd try to memorize the steps, locate a pattern, crack the code. And in the midst of counting workers landing, *eleven, twelve, thirteen,* I'd confuse the number with back steps of the dancer—a twirl, a pause, a right turn—then look up as they flew away, longing to go with them to see if they'd find the field of iris in bloom. At night I put my ear to the side of the hive to hear the purring of wings fanning to evaporate liquid and keep the brood's temperature on an even keel. Mid-July when it was still eighty at night, their increasing numbers became more evident. Many excused their body heat from the mix by hanging out on the front porch, and as the weeks passed, they began to cover the ledge and drip down the sides, clinging in thick masses to the cement blocks, which supported their home like ivy growing up a brick wall.

A second brood box and shallow super were added just about the time the nectar flow ended, and all vegetation turned a crisp brown. I walked the two-mile radius surrounding our house, the general limit of foraging bees' range only to find that cattle had stripped leaves from lower branches and blooms of any kind had shriveled and died. My wife watered the few flowering plants in our yard, but there's no guarantee a bee will draw nectar from any given source, and the beds we had could scarcely support a booming hive. Leaves began to fall in early August, and we didn't see rain for the rest of the year. Fortunately bees can locate nectar sources better than I, and they continued to forage; the queen continued her methodical laying of eggs. In September I opened the hive—the bottom super was completely drawn out, and the frames were honey heavy; a few in the second story were drawn out but held only empty cells; the frames in the third story hadn't been touched. I left what honey there was for their winter sustenance.

Heavy rains came with April, and with it, a river of nectar. I imagined pulling homemade biscuits from the oven in the fall and slathering them with rich, dark honey. Then we bought a house ten miles down the road, and I moved the hive late at night by myself in eighty-degree weather, jostling and jarring it in and out of the truck. A keeper knows his limits and seeks help from others, but I was in a rush to get the job done. As a result, most of the colony swarmed overnight, and I was left with another weak hive, another year with no hope for honey, another year as just one who has bees.

The intangibles were still there with an added benefit—I had learned to mark when plants flowered and pollen rained from trees. I'd lived in Texas twenty years, and until I kept bees, didn't know what mesquite trees looked like in bloom. Fifteen crepe myrtles lined the front of our new house, and when they bloomed, my wife and I stood beneath the branches listening to them buzz. We bought two birdbaths—one with an angel centerpiece, the other with a little girl—and the bees began to congregate by the water, resting on the hems of the statues' robes.

Quite a change from this afternoon when bees hung like storm clouds, nearly indistinguishable from the smoke emanating from the roaring fire I'd built fifty feet from the hives, and the smoke that rolled from the tops of the hives, and the shroud of smoke I was engulfed in from the constant cranking of the bellows, on my clothes, in my veil to ward off attacks that came like lightning strikes. I paced from hive to fire, weighing each frame, tossing ones that only held bees into the flames, brushing more into the air if the frame was heavy with honey. A keeper removes a frame slowly to avoid rolling the bees, but I pried the frames from the box with much jiggling and movement because the quicker I could get them to the fire, the sooner this unpleasant task would be complete. By the time I made it to the bottom supers, I'd pull a frame, and my head would be covered. The bees were like metal, drawn to a magnetic veil. They sounded like buckshot flung off a tin roof.

This morning I had expected the hives to be desolate, given the gray bodies that lined the ledges and lay in small heaps on the ground, the chalky dust and curled insects I encountered when I lifted the tops, and the general inactivity I'd witnessed for a month or more. The roar that sounded when I cracked the first inner cover disabused me of that notion, though the top super was near empty and calm. A few frames were partially drawn out but no honey. I placed these on the ground. The second layer was crawling with bees, and as I tried to peer to the bottom of the hive between the frames, my vision was blocked by a mass of comb and sluggish-moving bodies. The mistake I'd made was not taking winter into consideration. The previous two years have been an endless summer—one-hundred-plus temperatures for two or three months broken by months in the sixties and seventies, a few weeks in the fifties, a night of heavy frost. This winter, though, we've had freezing weather, icy wind days, and weeks without sun. I'd had no experience with bees in cold weather. They weren't dead, only huddled together conserving heat. I could have taken this knowledge, turned back, closed the hives, waited one more year in the hope they'd produce. I now know why murder comes in degrees, why pre-meditated acts receive a more harsh penalty. Once you've made up your mind, the deed has already been done.

And my mind was made up eight months ago when I opened the lid of the hive I'd combined with the swarm, removed shreds of newspaper that remained, witnessed no great struggle between workers, and began to feel pretty good about myself as a keeper of bees: it was time to split the colonies. I pieced together two brood boxes and four shallow supers during the evenings of the following weeks. The wood had been shipped pre-cut, complete with notched ends and the appropriate nails. Hitting the nail on the head, dead center, to drive it perfectly straight was a must given the ½" x ½" face of each notch. Once the boxes were together, I nailed the thin metal strips along the inside ridge of each end piece that would maintain the appropriate bee space between frames, slapped paint on the outside, left them to dry and began putting together frames. The construction of each frame required several steps: I joined the soft pine bottom and top bars with an end piece using nails roughly the size of an eye lash, slid a thin plastic support into the grooves along the insides of the frame, sandwiched the plastic with sheets of wax, and nailed the other end tight. Wax warps during the process, especially when the last end piece is secured, so the bubbles had to be subdued with a furious fingernail. A few split ends, a smattering of goddamns, and a bruised thumb later, I'd knocked together sixty frames and had two new complete hives.

Much of which this afternoon I dismantled and shook and burned.

The risk of splitting a strong colony is that you replace it with two that are weak, but I desperately wanted two hives. I had equipment for two hives. I had captured a swarm with the express purpose of creating two hives.

THE RISK INVOLVED

Drifting among bees—confusion over which hive is theirs—occurs when hives sit side by side, so to avoid this I placed the new brood box on the opposite side of the laundry room adjacent to the propane tank with the mouth of the hive facing away from the back door in hopes they'd establish flight patterns that didn't involve our major walkways. I removed four frames from the middle to be replaced with frames from the old hive heavy with honey and brood. Both hives could be split fairly equally in this regard, although initially all field bees would return to the original hive. One hive, however, would experience a few weeks of autonomy since it would operate without a queen.

A trained keeper's eye can sift through frames in the brood box and identify her, but I've tried on several occasions and have never successfully found the bee with an elongated body laying eggs. Fortunately I found plenty of queen cells—dark bulges that hang near the bottom of a frame. Ordinarily queen cells are bad news—an indication that the queen is weak or old, and the workers are raising a new one, while others are preparing to pack up and leave with the old one. But for one who just keeps bees, it was an opportunity to make sure whichever hive ended up in anarchy could raise a new monarch within a short period of time. And it did. Both hives built up significant numbers through the summer despite the drought-like conditions. And last August, once again, I carefully pried open both lids and found that none of the shallow supers had been drawn out. Another year with no excess honey.

Reasons for destroying a hive are few. American foulbrood, chalk and bald brood, wax moths and nematodes, fire ants, mites and beetles—a host of parasites and disease left undetected, neglected, and untreated—can decimate a colony to the point of extinction. In rare cases such as foulbrood, the hive must be destroyed. Natural remedies have been purported to work for the most pressing threat to the modern hive—Tracheal and Varroa mites. Periodically, I crushed rosemary and peppermint essential oil into the sugar-water solution. The bees consumed this mixture more slowly, but it's supposed to kill mites on contact, even discourage their reproduction if the bees use the seasoned sugar to draw out foundation in the hive. A friend found research that suggested painting one's hive black increased the bees' body temperature enough to kill the mites. But I had already painted selected brood boxes with a dull gray, interspersed them with white ones for more aesthetic appeal. If these chem-free remedies worked, I wouldn't really know; I never conducted tests that would reveal the presence of mites. However, if I ever had honey to sell, I could guarantee that it was not only fresh, but also 100% chemical free.

Another reason to destroy a hive arises only in northern climes. A colony can maintain limited numbers in the most dire of conditions. I've seen pictures of hives buried in six feet of snow. The bees clump around the queen, and though many perish, a hive usually bounces back with the spring thaw. Starting the season with weak hives, though, makes them susceptible to robbing and disease, and so keepers in areas with particularly harsh winters, subzero temperatures for months on end, will destroy all their colonies after the autumn harvest, order new queens and package bees, and begin anew every year. The practice is controversial, or so the southern keepers I've talked to say.

Destroying a colony simply because they're aggressive or low honey producers isn't a common practice either. Keepers simply re-queen the hive, by locating the old one, killing her, and introducing a new one. Since the queen is the sole provider of offspring, within a short period of time, the entire hives' genetic makeup changes (for the better, hopefully). One can even change the strain of their hive over a short period of time by introducing a queen of a different type. I considered re-queening our hives after the second year with no honey but decided the intangibles were still enough to justify them in our lives. And then the relationship changed a bit; in the third year, they began to show an aggression I hadn't yet seen.

Our small mutt, Rudy, liked to sit quietly to the side of the hive and lick unsuspecting bees off the ledge when they landed. Dogs are genetically similar to bears, and so they're bees' sworn enemies. He usually got nailed on his tongue or the roof of his mouth, occasionally on the nose or eyelid, so he never made off with enough to make an appreciable difference. One afternoon, he tagged along while I refilled the feeders. A few trackers whipped around the hive after I replaced the full jar and buzzed my head and face. I went to the work shed to clean up and lost track of Rudy, until I heard him barking on the front porch. My wife let him in and returned moments later yelling from the porch, "the dog's buzzing." I ran inside and chased him down with a towel while Christa drew water in the tub. We picked over twenty bees from his thick fur and crushed them in the towel. I'm not certain how many times he was stung, but other than looking hangdog for the rest of the day, he was fine.

After we'd plucked the last bee from the dog, I still heard buzzing so went to investigate. The dog had run under the bed when he'd first made it inside, and the ones he'd shaken off had gravitated to the sunlight of the window. I carefully opened the mini-blinds on both windows and counted an additional fifteen to twenty on each. An occasional bee has made it indoors every month or so from the first day we got them. I always take a plastic cup, carefully scoop the intruder inside, and release her back outside. That afternoon, though, I picked up one of Christa's white Keds and began to whack. Crushed bodies hung on the glass, and a few fell crumpled to the sill. It was the first time I'd actively sought them out for destruction. Perhaps it was the sheer volume and logistical challenge of taking them out one-by-one, or maybe because they'd swarmed our dog, who is indeed like a child to us, even though he was long overdue for retaliation. Regardless, a shift had occurred in our relationship with the bees. And I felt uneasy and sad.

A week later Christa was out washing her car, and she rushed inside to announce, "they're after me." I stood on the front porch and watched a small swarm dive-bombing the soapy bucket and stream of water from the leaking hose. Their numbers had increased to the point where every path around our house was in a direct flight line. Walking to the truck each morning, to the garden or compost pile in the evening, sitting on the porch to read or hanging out clothes, I'd get buzzed. I got stung reaching to turn off the spigot one evening and then a few weeks later was nearly engulfed with bees while chipping branches in the side yard with my shredder. I stepped back and watched as hundreds of bees gathered above the chipper, floating and dipping toward the motor as though the machine were manufacturing bees and spewing them into the air. I got suited up in my bee gear and killed the engine. A few hours later I returned to rake leaves for a while to shred on a more cloudy day when the familiar angry buzz caused me to raise my arm too late, and I was nailed beneath my left eye.

And so, one night just before dark, I measured the length of the hive entrances, cut two pieces of wood and wrapped them both with wire mesh. After the sun set, we smoked the bees inside both hives and wedged the wood and wire into the entrance. I pulled the truck around the house and backed it up as close to the hive sitting on the south side of the laundry room as I could. The hive probably weighed about fifty or sixty pounds, well within Christa's and my ability to lift, but a hive is an awkward piece of bulk that offers no easy grip. Nonetheless we dropped the tailgate and lugged both hives to the truck and sat them on the edge. Christa then followed behind, balancing the hives as I drove at a snail's pace to the far side of the yard. Unloading proved to be more difficult, but we reset the cement blocks and laid them in place. We only own an acre of land, and the hives were still on it, but it felt like the bees weren't as much a part of our lives. We placed them as close to the fence as possible, so that there was just enough room to walk around at a safe distance. We continued to visit them on a daily basis, but there had just been something near magical about walking out the back door and immediately being greeted by the activity and buzz.

THE RISK INVOLVED

I've told you all of this, so it doesn't appear that I'm hiding anything. Yes, there have been problems with the bees. Yes, I've been stung numerous times; yes, my wife has been chased around the yard; yes, the dog has been covered, and they've invaded our house. Yes, we've brought this upon ourselves: the dog by thinking they were snacks, my wife and me for bringing them into our lives and planting them too near our back door, and me for running heavy equipment that vibrates within close proximity of their home. And since the bees can't speak for themselves, I'll say this on their behalf—they've only acted according to their nature to protect themselves, protect the brood, protect the queen, protect the hive—give their life for the good of the cause.

A keeper becomes attached to a species, a distinct colony as a whole. Not a single worker or drone remained from the original box of bees I picked up from the post office three years ago. Neither queen might be the original, even though they can live up to seven years. During the winter when the work load is light, workers usually live to see the new year, a few to celebrate the Mardi Gras, but the sun up, sun down toil that comes with the nectar flow will fray their wings, zap their strength, and drive them to an early grave within a span of four to six weeks. A healthy hive regenerates at such a rapid rate in such astounding volume that no one's death seems to diminish the whole. Bees haven't the time to mourn. This doesn't give a keeper the right to destroy them en masse in one afternoon or suggest that just because their span is brief, they don't scurry, lash, and cling in an effort to protect the hive, even if it means delivering the sting that seals the bee's own death warrant.

My wife and I planned on re-queening our hives later this spring, but then our lives took a turn—we've been married seven years, lived in the same area, and had the same jobs for five—wanderlust began to creep into our thoughts and conversations. We started to make plans. We've talked of returning to Kentucky to experience seasons once again, where white clover grows in abundance, and beekeeping is good. Or perhaps to Ft. Worth where my parents live, where my sister just had a baby, the first of a new generation. Or maybe Louisiana where Christa's parents live. Then a job opportunity opened that would require me starting in a matter of weeks. Our idle talk set us in motion. We decided not to move the bees.

Destroying them seemed like a good idea until I encountered a frame heavy with honey. Christa was watching from a distance so I told her what I'd found. She went in the house and grabbed a cookie sheet while I carried the full frame to the fire and started brushing off the bees. It was a messy business. Over the next several hours I sifted through both hives, setting empty frames to the side, carrying frames heavy with bees but void of honey to be destroyed in the fire, and frames heavy with both to the fire where I tried to separate the two. Since destruction was my only goal, I began plucking bees from my veil and crushing them between my leather-covered fingers. Several, who had gorged themselves from being smoked oozed, honey when crushed.

Once we had the frames inside, we began the honey retrieval. Various fancy tools exist for honey extraction—electric knives for de-capping and honey spinners—but since we hadn't planned on harvesting any honey, we were caught unprepared. However, for the small volume we had, common kitchen utensils would do. We boiled two long knives in water and used them to skim across the top of the full frames, just to remove the wax caps and expose the honey. Then we cut sections of the comb and placed them upside down in a sieve. Once a few combs had drained, I squeezed them to remove the excess honey, and we commenced to cutting more. We placed a few sections of combs into jars. The knives needed to be re-heated after several cuttings and the honey drained slow in the sieve, and the sieve was small, so the task took several hours. We tried a blow dryer for a while to make the honey flow faster, and while this worked immediately, it soon began to melt the wax, which plugged up the sieve and ultimately made the process slower. Near the end, I'd simply squeeze the comb over the sieve—much got trapped in the wax ball, so a bit was wasted, but as often as not, I plopped the mass into my mouth, sucked the honey dry, and chewed on the wax until it fell apart in my mouth.

In all, we garnered nearly two gallons of honey. A paltry amount from two hives, thousands of bees, and three years—but it tasted sweet, nonetheless. It tasted sweet on my fingers and melting in a cup of hot tea. And the memories were sweet of the excitement I felt the day I drove furiously on my lunch break to the post office to pick up my first package of bees, the visits with the old man in Austin whom I bought my first hive from, the late afternoons Christa and I sat in lawn chairs watching them bring pollen home, the spiraling dance when they swarmed, and their sweet buzz in the crepe myrtle trees. Tonight, though, I'm not so sure I'll sleep so well with the fire still smoldering and the smoke clinging dense to my dreams.

INDEFINITE LIGHT

Christmas Eve, and the nativities I visited with my wife and her family were triangular log constructions perched along the levee's edge. One hundred and sixty in all. We had hoods and stocking caps pulled over our ears, disguising us as much as the light mist and darkness. The incline to reach the levee's peak was steep, as these manmade mounds were constructed to keep floodwaters at bay, the neighborhoods safe a hundred yards from their base, and not so much as pleasant walkways for folks on holiday. Two days of wispy rain and temperatures in the forties (enough in the South to call a white Christmas) made the ascent precarious—that, and a few cups of hurricane punch.

Barges, hidden by darkness, ran the Mississippi and sounded their foghorns at seven to give signal to the bonfires' builders, who distinguished themselves by emerging with lighters and matches to strike the first tiny flares into the night, to ignite torches they used to set the levee ablaze. The diesel-soaked logs flashed and, for a second, seemed to lift off the ground as though they were fiery chariots heaven-bound, but it's nothing that sacred: it's a celebration for children who know nothing of death, who believe they're lighting the way through the fog and mist for Saint Nicklaus. This is Lutcher, Louisiana. Christmas Eve in the South.

THE RISK INVOLVED

We wandered to the canal that separates levee from water to escape the great heat and stray bottle rockets, the crackling of cane that adorns many structures, and this is what we saw: the obvious line of bonfires that began with the closest flames stretched to the black sky thirty feet or more and moved to seemingly smaller structures until the burning logs diminished into camp fire sizes, and then luminaries, and then candle light, until the capacity to see even night fires failed. Yet we lingered longer and endured the cold, resisted the temptation to return to the heat, until our eyes adjusted to the contrast of darkness punctured by light, and in the shadows we saw human figures in clusters with appendages of children, extended family members, along with close friends.

The construction on bonfires begins late in October when families and friends cut trees from their woods, strip off the branches on tailgates of trucks, measure and saw the logs into sections, haul them by flat bed, load after load, to the edge of the levee where larger logs used for the base are pulled up the slope by four-wheeler and tractor while those for the frame are hand-carried by two or more women and men. The top pieces that will be placed later by ladder are carried by children who treat them like stars. The logs are then placed end over end to create box upon box of diminishing size, spiraling upward until pyramids twenty-five feet tall begin to take shape, each one composed of hundreds of parts. Not an afternoon's work, but two months of weekends and the builders claim their structures are sturdy as houses, and that on Christmas morn one can look out the window and still see them smoldering all along the high ridge.

A century-old tradition passed down through generations naturally brings out attempts to make one's structure unique, and while most take the typical shape, there are variations—Cajun cabins and deer stands, staircases, log houses, oil rig towers manned by plastic Santa Clauses. Some are covered in cane that pops when ignited, others strung with firecrackers whose gun powder explosions send a succession of echoes across the water and back. Banners hang from a few with football team logos, proclamations for Jesus or someone not as well known, but when the fires are lit, they're caught in the updraft, flapping and curled, sending bits of burning cloth into the air like fiery moths. And no matter the cold shape of individual structures, all these yuletide offerings are reduced to ash, taken by the wind that mingles them together, ushers them away along with the old year.

Community, then, is missing the game's second half, Thanksgiving afternoon, to walk through the forest picking out perfect trees. The sharpening of handsaws and demonstrations for children of the blade's proper angle when pruning a branch. Watching old men wielding chainsaws without binding the blade. The loss of Sunday naptime to push trucks out of mud, enjoying lukewarm thermos coffee while the radiator cools. Enduring blisters and sore backs, scratched faces and arms, taking two aspirin before bedtime washed down with a beer. All this for the creation of something you'll destroy in celebration because you know the reward for working together is time spent with people who raised you or saved you or who now call you "daddy" or whom you married or once dated, divorced but stayed friends, people whose secrets you're probably a part of, whose past is your own, whose voices sound the same, people you eat with, work for, commune with, get drunk with laughter come Saturday nights, people who seem unbearable at times but whose presence you can't imagine living without.

The miracle of this event is not a community of people; it's that they pull it off without sponsored bonfires or chain-link fences surrounding the grounds, gates manned by volunteers in matching attire taking seven bucks (one off for cola cans). No handstamps ready to prove that you were here, to allow you to return if you forgot something in the car. No fire or policemen waiting in the wings in case the people or the fires rage out of control. No lines to purchase tickets to wait in other lines to purchase meat on a stick to eat while waiting in other lines to purchase plastic cups of beer, flat, warm, and over-priced. It's bring your own everything— lawn chairs and umbrellas. Ice chests full of glass. No restrictions on fireworks or any dogs on leashes. Not a single sign to remind us how decent humans act. There was an older couple at a table across the road selling bonfire ornaments, t-shirts, and coffee mugs, but when we asked for different sizes, the man shrugged and said, "I've got some at the house," as though we knew just where he lived and later could stop by.

We did stop by an open house for gumbo and headcheese, hosted by a couple who welcome friends and strangers every Christmas Eve. I still don't know who knew whom but took a steaming bowl, chased some boudin and pickled okra down with dark-spiced rum. There was karaoke in the living room, someone singing Elvis-style to his sweetheart about it being Christmastime and there's snow. Late that night back in Baton Rouge at a candlelight church service, we sang hymns and carols, listened to the Christmas story, and it felt right to be there for the first time in years. Perhaps it started on the levee or midway through a hurricane, my arms around my wife, her family standing near, or with the primeval draw of fire, the first great gift of gods, or this rediscovery of community, four hundred miles from where I live. Perhaps it's just Christmas Eve, but I thought how wonderful it would be if everything in this evening was all anyone could need.

The news the night before showed a stable-shaped bonfire complete with plastic, life-size Mary, Joseph, and the Child surrounded by sheep, shepherds, and angels illumined by floodlight. The story, as it often is, was the commercialization of Christmas, and they showed images of Santas towered over nativities, the man on the street bemoaning what it has become, and last minute shoppers maxing out their credit cards. The price exacted for living makes this existence painful, almost surreal, and while I haven't an idea how it should be, this is what I know: a secular blend with the sacred—inferno nativities to light the way for jolly 'ole Saint Nick may be crass at best, but any version of a thing that causes wonder and joy is worthy of celebration, is another form of prayer. This I also know: the moment the barge horns sounded and the fires caught complete, they seemed to suck air from our lungs, leaving us mute at flashpoint, but our voices soon returned with a chorus of fireworks, as though something had been accomplished, as though we, with frozen breath and numb fingers, had called the fires forth.

WALK AWAY SLOWLY (YOU KNOW YOU'LL BE BACK)

A single bee, bouncing along a sunlit window, searching for an egress, would not be cause for alarm; however, five, six, seven bees in one spot near the floor suggests I'm looking at the entrance to a hive. Bees crawl in and out of an electrical socket, and I know the wise thing to do is call an exterminator and a carpenter. I crouch a few feet closer for a better look and see the outlet cover is slightly askew, creating a gap that has allowed them into this Sunday School room which, as I understand it, has not been used in decades. The building is fifty, sixty years old. The church is dying. These bees are not lost; they're taking over.

"I might need to cut into the wall a little," I say to the church president who is fidgeting behind me in the doorway. He's one of my neighbors, a somewhat nervous man, in general, who talks rapid-fire with lots of hand gestures. Today he is even more fidgety than usual. He does not share my infatuation with bees.

"I just want the bees gone," he says.

"Might take a few hours," I say.

"I'll leave you to it," he says. And he does.

I suspect these Sunday School bees have a well-established hive in the wall, a removal job better suited for a professional beekeeper. I am a recovering salesman who recently worked his way back into academia, teaching remedial writing classes. My credentials for bee-removals is limited to keeping hives as a hobby years ago, and my last bee interaction involved me destroying my hives because I was moving to a cul-de-sac in the suburbs. It's a memory I'd prefer to erase; however, I've never lost the inexplicable desire to handle stinging insects.

Seven years ago, my wife and I moved back to a small town, and the only reason anyone here knows I'm infatuated with bees is because I joined the Kiwanis club, and part of each member's responsibilities is to provide, twice a year, an after-lunch program on some topic. My first time around, I presented on the importance of Long-Term Care Insurance. A few months later, I had a better read on the room: nobody in the club is trying to sell anything because they all already do business with one another. Therefore, I decided to share an essay I'd written about catching a swarm of bees. Since then, several times each spring, someone will call for advice on buzzing sounds in bedroom walls, hives spilling from backlot tree trunks, or swarms tucked in old tractor tires. What people in town don't realize is I am better with words than I am with bees. And yet, even when I know the odds are against me successfully eradicating their insect problems, I can't resist the desire to give it a shot because I am hopelessly addicted to enterprises involving chance.

"I'm just gonna take a look," I'll tell my wife when someone calls about bees.

"Can you get to them?" she'll ask.

"Not sure," I'll say.

"Take a Benadryl," she'll say.

"I've just gotta see."

I am allergic to bee stings and, in theory, could die of anaphylactic shock if careless. It's been years since my wife had to rush me to the hospital as my head swelled from a bee misadventure, but since then, I minimize the risk by popping antihistamines, wearing protective clothing, and assessing weather and location of swarms.

It's a bit like playing poker: never leave the house with more money than you're willing to lose, learn the habits of other players, and always drive yourself to the game so you avoid gambling drunk.

Sometimes, though, you just have to fold and walk away like the nights when the guy across the table keeps raising your bets and hitting on the river card. Or when a guy calls you with a colony of bees who've made their home in an abandoned hot water heater.

"I've got a blowtorch," the guy said. We were standing in his backfield on the edge of his junk pile, watching bees creep in and out of the heater's drainpipe.

"Yeah, I don't know," I said.

"Stupid idea," he said.

"Probably."

I ran into him a few months later, and he told me he'd waited until dusk on a night we were expecting a hard freeze.

"I filled the tank with water and capped it off," he said.

I winced.

"You probably didn't want to hear that."

"Sometimes you gotta do what you gotta do," I said.

That night I dreamt of frozen bees.

The downside of walking away too many times is the gnawing regret of missed opportunity. *What if we had given the blowtorch a shot?*

In many variations of poker, the dealer initially gives you two cards that only you see. As the hand progresses, you receive more cards with which to string together a (hopefully) competitive hand. However, on the first round, you are betting on the potential of these two cards. Allegedly, the worst opening hand you can be dealt is an unsuited two and nine; it's called "the hammer." Conventional wisdom says it's an easy fold. That said, players have won several high-stakes poker tournaments with the hammer. I, myself, have won a few hands by ultimately doubling up with two pairs by the time all the cards were on the table. And therein lies the problem: sure, you can lose with a crummy hand, but you can never win if you walk away. There's always a chance.

THE RISK INVOLVED

The rewards for taking a chance capturing a swarm and establishing them on your own property is standing over an open hive, peering into a mass of beautiful insects who are vibrating with the joy of work. Or sitting at a distance with binoculars, watching a bee on the hive ledge performing an intricate dance that serves as a map for other bees to find flowers or water. Or, if I'm really lucky, catching a glimpse of a bee returning to the hive with yellow and pink pollen pellets tucked into her back legs.

I walk outside to the back of the building to investigate where the bees are getting in; however, a wall of saplings and waist-high weeds make it near impossible to get close. I'd much rather cut holes on an exterior wall, but hacking through all the brush would eat up most of the morning. This will have to be an inside job. I am on Fall Break, a wonderful luxury of higher education designed to give students a mid-semester breather from classes and faculty a chance to catch up on grading. It's been over a decade since I've taught, so I've been behind since day one. I've allowed myself this single Tuesday morning to play with bees. Whatever challenges lie ahead, though, beats repeatedly marking comma splices, run-on sentences, and word choices. By a freaking mile.

After I destroyed my hives, I had misgivings about continuing to consider myself a hobby beekeeper; the fact that this morning, I easily located my veil, leather gloves, smoker, and hive tool (a small crowbar with razor-sharp ends) in the garage suggests I have never completely given up on the idea. It all came back in a rush: I knocked cockroaches out of an old, deep super (the bigger boxes at the bottom of hives where bees store brood and honey), and found a few intact wax frames. I scrounged a roll of screen, duct tape, newspaper, and wood chips for the smoker. I also grabbed my drill and reciprocating saw—not the normal tools in a beekeeper's kit and probably a tangible sign that I should abort this mission.

I also have a nagging concern that even if I successfully remove bees from the wall, my backyard isn't ideal. While we live in a residential area, and the lot is large enough to house a hive tucked in the far corner of the yard, the only thing separating our lawn from an elementary school across the street is our waist-high picket fence. We also have three young children of our own. I can't shake the image of schoolchildren on the merry-go-round, surrounded by a cloud of swarming bees.

That said, the church president is also one of my neighbors. He and his wife own the oldest pharmacy in town. Their people have lived in this town for generations. If my residential beekeeping goes sideways, I can always deflect blame onto pillars of the community.

Back in the Sunday School room, I carefully unscrew the wall plate. Dozens of bees spill out. The telltale hum, indicating an established colony within the wall, grows louder. A thin line of honey oozes from the crack between the outlet box and the wall. It is, at once, thrilling and deflating. I had a dim hope this was a recent swarm—an aging queen and a group of workers who have left a crowded hive in search of a new home. In theory, a swarm is an easy group to corral and re-establish in a backyard hive. They are more docile because they don't have brood (eggs, larvae, and pupae) or food to protect. The fact that honey is dripping from the socket suggests these bees have been here for months, maybe years, and are going to be unwilling to accept my invitation to move.

If I am able to cut out a portion of the wall, locate the queen and scoop her into the deep super, then I can walk away for several hours. Worker bees are hardwired to forage pollen, make honey, fend off hive predators, and protect the queen. If you put a queen in a box, eventually all the workers will cluster around her. Search the internet for "bee beard" if you want to see a dramatic (and ill-advised) example of how this works. While I have never hazarded this trick, I have successfully captured two swarms. I have also failed at numerous attempts and been stung multiple times in the process.

I duct tape the bottom of my pant legs to my leather boots and do the same around the top of my elbow-length gloves. For good measure,

THE RISK INVOLVED

I wrap some tape around the bottom mesh of my bee veil as well. Head coverings for keepers come in different styles, and mine is a lightweight screen veil that slips over the top of a plastic safari helmet. I've never owned a full bee suit because old folks at beekeeping meetings insist that a veil and common sense is all you need if you know what you're doing. Just in case, I also have thermal underwear on beneath my long-sleeve cotton shirt. I've also eaten a few antihistamines because sometimes it's wise to compensate for lack of experience with a bit of caution. It's also why I try to drink less when there's an old man at the poker table.

Sweat trickles down my forehead as I tap the area above the outlet with my hive tool, trying to determine where to make the initial cut. This building's construction predates sheetrock, a material I've always thought a sad substitute for lath and plaster or solid wood, but I'm starting to appreciate how much easier it would be to access the bees through a more pliable surface. I can't determine where the comb ends and the hollow recess of the interior wall begins. Sometimes you just have to jump in with both feet. Drill in hand.

Even if you've never considered ripping bees from a wall, you instinctively suspect punching a drill bit into this wood is not the wisest thing I will do today. The corkscrew intrusion is one thing, but what concerns me most is that bees detest the hum of machinery. Back when I kept three hives on my property, bees would pelt me if I got too close with a lawn mower or wood chipper. When riled, they attack the equipment and the operator with equal ferocity. Let's face it, though: nobody likes somebody else messing with their home.

Even though I believe what I am doing for the bees will make their lives better (better, at least, than an exterminator would), forging a relationship with insects is not the same as adopting a puppy from the animal shelter. If bees remain on your property in manufactured hives you've provided, it's because there are adequate pollen and water sources nearby, the area is not damp, and fire ant activity is minimal. Bees will never grow to love you.

I do believe, however, they can grow to hate you.

I place the bit about a foot above the socket and drill the first hole. Honey immediately oozes down the wall. A second hole, two feet above the first, produces more honey. I am farther up the wall than I want to be but still not high enough to clear the comb. The bees in the room are not unruly, but they are becoming agitated. *You think you're nervous*, I tell them as I switch out the drill for the reciprocating saw. The dull blade bites into the hardwood, and my arms shake along with the first jolting cut. Apparently, there are horizontal boards bracing the entirety of these walls, so I'm cutting through wood all the way down. Not only is the machine vibrating, but the entire wall is shaking as well. I can't hear the bees within the wall over all the racket I'm making, but I can assure you the sound they are making is unsettling.

The bees rolling out of the bottom of the wall are increasing in frequency like bubbles forming on the bottom of a pot of boiling water. The more I cut, the more bubbles appear. I imagine the water's surface where bubbles swell and pop is level with my head. As I cut through the final side of the rectangle and pull away the section of wood, the bees have reached a roiling boil. I am neck-deep in hot bees.

If a bee has approached you outdoors, you may have found the encounter startling, but if you remained composed, surely you noticed bees appear to be floating more than flying. They are aeronautical wonders, shifting in flight so quickly they seem to appear and disappear like blinking lights. And, I am not the first to imagine, that if we could see notes of music being played, they would look exactly like bees. The lilt of a bee in flight is pure joy.

If, on the other hand, you have just disturbed a hive with a reciprocating saw, the flight of the bee is very different. I am uncertain if they actually roll themselves into a ball, or if their ability to double the speed at which they move whips them into small spheres, but I do know when they hit the screen of my veil, it sounds like I've been shot with a pellet gun. Angry bees are always aiming for your eyes because somewhere in the dark shadows of their evolutionary past, their wise ancestors discovered pricking bears' eyeballs was an effective way to make predators tumble.

Fortunately I, too, learned something from my shadowy beekeeping past: there's a moment in every bee interaction when it's time to walk away.

I am stung on my neck and forearm, which means despite my layers of clothing and duct tape, several bees have worked their way through gaps and folds to lance my skin. The retribution is fair, more than fair, as you might recall bees sting once only. After the stinger lodges into your skin and the bee pulls away, the action disembowels her and, shortly after, she dies. Their commitment to the good of the community is something I admire but am too selfish to comprehend completely.

My bee smoker has been smoldering in the corner since I started drilling, and I grab it, squeezing the bellows to generate large clouds of smoke, which is supposed to calm bees; however, I am pouring it on thick in an attempt to choke the bees clinging to me. In the process, of course, I am smoking the hell out of my eyes and lungs. As a last resort, just as I am about to open the door to escape, I swat and kill the remaining bees on my arms and legs. A squashed bee releases a scent that serves as an alarm to other bees, which is why, ordinarily, you should avoid killing them, but none of that matters now since my sawing already set off the equivalent of bells, whistles, and flashing lights.

Once outside, I check myself for lingering bees, swatting and shooing before whipping off the veil and gloves, collapsing on my tailgate, and hoping for a breeze. This reminds me too much of my last bee encounter when I destroyed my hives. The excessive smoke I puffed around my head and torso, coupled with the sweat running down my face, has left my eyes red and stinging.

JEFFREY UTZINGER

There comes a time in every gambler's life when they question the wisdom of their chosen pastime, when they find themselves throwing good money after bad cards, when a voice in their head says *walk away*. The reward for staying the course, though, is the thrill of peering over a table covered with red, white, and blue chips scattered amongst diamonds, the queen of hearts, a suicide jack, and the king of spades. And the experience of losing track of time, drinking, engaged in meaningless small talk and a game that lends itself to suspense but is based on repetition, set rules, and clear winners and losers. And, if you're really lucky, calling an all-in bet, hitting a full house on the river, and raking in several hundred dollars' worth of chips.

I learned to play poker in college, but when I moved to this town, I learned how to gamble. I'd met a few guys my age, married with small children, all of us relatively new to small-town living. Some of us were looking for social groups, people we could eventually turn into clients; some of us wanted an evening away from bedtime stories; some of us were just lonely, nostalgic for late nights in dorms. It started when four or five of us gathered in someone's dining room to learn Texas Hold 'Em, a hundred-year-old game that was experiencing a renaissance due to expanded television coverage of the World Series of Poker. That night, we spent an hour learning the rules, showing each other our cards, asking questions, and drinking a lot of beer. Then, we played a winner-take-all tournament for nickels, dimes, and quarters.

That first night, it all came down to two players and one final deal. I turned the corner on a ten and a four, unsuited—not the worst hole hand in poker, but close. My oldest daughter, however, was born on the tenth day of the fourth month. I took it as a sign, and did not fold. The flop also contained a ten and a four. I don't recall if I, or my opponent, went "all in," but one of us called, which meant all of our money was on the table. The turn card didn't help me, but the river was another ten, which gave me a full house—not the best hand in poker but pretty close. I won the night and a bulging pocket of change. I also learned two things: if you stay in long enough, almost any hand can be a winner, and while winning is always better than losing, I am addicted most to the thrill of risking it all on the promise of one card.

As I sit on my tailgate waiting for the Sunday School bees to settle down so I can cut another section from the wall, I know the odds are this bee recovery is going to be a disaster. However, in poker, there's often a moment between rounds of betting that you realize you no longer, statistically, have a winning hand. There are too many potential straights, flushes, or full houses showing on the table, and the most you can hit is two pair. However, you've already called too many bets—have too much money in the pot—to fold. You are, what they call, "pot committed." I have damaged too much of the wall and carpet, been stung too many times, invested too much of my morning to just call an exterminator and a carpenter. These bees and I might not like it, but we're in this together. Win, lose, or draw.

It's close to lunchtime, but there's a knot in my stomach, and I'm too grimy to consider eating. About an hour has passed, so I pull on my equipment, reapply duct tape, stuff more woodchips into the smoker, and head back inside where I am immediately greeted by several bees; they're not pelting me like before, but they are weaving around my head. I send light puffs of smoke around the room like I'm performing a sage cleansing ritual even though this place reeks of morning after campfire. I slide open the windows and push out part of the screen. Anyone who wishes to escape is welcome. A slow stream of honey still flows down the walls, pooling on the floor, where bees are in recovery mode, sucking up the liquid to return to their hive. They look like tubers on a Spring Break river. Or miniature cattle grazing at the water's edge. Maybe Sisyphus with little balls of honey, blissfully unaware of how gravity works. I've stalled enough. It's time to crank up the machinery.

I quickly drill two holes at eye level and start cutting a six-inch by two-inch rectangle out of the wall. The bees converge immediately. An hour ago, the vibrations disoriented the bees before whipping them into a raging whirlwind, but now they have a clear understanding of what's at stake. They're resolved: *This sonofabitch has got to go.*

The blade cuts through the final board, and I jump back. Broken wood, honey, comb, brood, and yes, more bees, erupt from the wall, cascading across the floor. I want to stop time and stand here to survey every detail of a six-foot tall beehive, deconstructed. Instead, I pull the deep super from the corner and start grabbing handfuls of bees. This might sound like an impossible task to perform without squashing the bees, but in a way, it's like scooping up water. The wonder of the human brain and hand/eye coordination is you instinctively know how much or how little pressure to apply. It's a sticky mess, however, because many are soaked in honey from the fall, but I'm able to fill the deep super in relatively short time.

I pump the smoker's bellows a few times, not really to calm anyone, but rather because I have to pick it up anyway and take it with me, so I don't set the carpet on fire. This day will be a total loss if I manage to burn down a Sunday School building in the process. I don't even bother brushing any bees off clothing this time since I am covered to my elbows in honey. One final puff and I'm out the door, slamming it behind me, running down the hallway to the main entrance, smoke and angry bees in my wake.

As I burst through the building's front door, a car passes by the church. The startled driver slows, and I wave in what I hope is a nonchalant, nothing-to-see-here, sort of way. I fully expect emergency vehicles to arrive soon.

While cooling down in the parking lot, I call the church president.

"You get 'em?" he asks.

"Getting close," I lie.

"Oh, okay."

"I've ruined the carpet," I say.

"Don't care. Just get the bees," he says.

"I'm headed home for a few more things." I pause a moment, not wanting to incite panic, but his pharmacy is just a few blocks from the church. He might get curious.

"You still there?" he asks.

"Whatever you do," I blurt out, "don't go in that room."

"Not enough money in the world," he says.

At home, I make a sandwich and eat it standing up. I feel bad even being in the house. We are by no means neat freaks; our home is seventy years old, decorated in what I call, Early American Yard Sale—antiques and worn-out furniture from neighbors, family, and friends. We also own roughly a million and one books (mainly my fault). We have three children under the age of ten, an indoor dog, and several indoor cats. If you could see me right now, however, you would wonder who thought it was a good idea to allow that filthy man to stand in their kitchen.

After eating, I stack half a flat of Mason jars on my shop vac, and load them into the truck.

The Sunday School room is still a flurry of activity, but the bees have settled somewhat because most of them are engaged in one of two pursuits: clustering around the deep super or gorging from the floor, which makes them more docile. They are trying to fill themselves as full as possible in order to return honey to what's left of the hive. A few bees are still on bear-eye-gouging duty, and as I move around the room, I am occasionally pelted.

A garland of bees hangs over the deep super's edge, and I gently wipe them inside so I can staple on a screen covering. No matter how fastidious one is in bee gathering, there are always a few left behind, and the stranglers will return to the comb fragments still clinging to the wall. Once a space has been used for a hive, especially in a wall or attic, it's near impossible to keep other bees from using it again because wax fuses with the porous wood. If you've ever tried to scrape candle drippings off a piece of furniture, you understand. A spot can be empty for months or years, but new bees can perceive the telltale signs: the slick wax residue, the lingering scent of honey and other bees, and of course, the qualities of the space—size, temperature, protection from predators—that attracted bees in the first place. This is why a carpenter is sometimes useful for bee removals because the best way to prevent return lodgers is to cut out and replace studs. All of this, of course, makes sense because humans do the same thing. Hence, cities built near rivers on top of ancient civilizations, and the modern real estate agents' mantra of *location, location, location.*

🐝 🐝 🐝

The draw of gambling works much the same way for those under its spell; it's near impossible to stay away if you know bets are being wagered in the neighborhood. I played poker with a friend's father-in-law who told me that, in his younger days, he lost so much money gambling, he asked all area casinos to ban him. My aunt and uncle lost two houses betting on Kentucky thoroughbreds. And, if you've ever been in a convenience store on the first of the month, you know it's quicker to pay at the pump than to wait in line behind people playing the numbers.

I never hit rock bottom but knew I was fooling myself justifying my habits by comparison. It was comforting to know someone who played more nights a week than I did, who stayed at the table longer, drank more, wagered and lost more. Comforting, that is, until I realized, some nights, I was becoming the "more than" guy.

The leap from a low-stakes, occasional game with a group of friends to playing several times a month, sometimes several times a week, happened because, at every table, every player was looking around, remembering faces and names in case sometime in the future they needed an extra guy for their monthly game.

For instance: a school board member stopped by my office for an insurance quote one afternoon, remembered me from a Chamber of Commerce Hold 'Em fundraiser, and asked what I was doing the next Thursday. He played in a monthly game with a bunch of coaches, teachers, school administrators, and their friends in a massive shed down by the river.

THE RISK INVOLVED

The first time I played in the river shed game, I saw a pastor I'd met at Kiwanis. He was kicked back at one of the tables on the other side of the room, smoking a cigar. The next week after Kiwanis, he and I happened to be walking out at the same time.

"I didn't know you played cards," I said.

"Jesus spent most of his time with prostitutes and tax collectors," he said.

"True enough," I said.

"Sometimes you've gotta go where the people are."

"Hey, I play a regular game, last Friday of every month."

"What time?" he asked.

In addition to these reoccurring games, guys would put together poker nights for birthdays or bachelor parties. Or sometimes, if you got knocked out of a tournament early, three or four other guys would be standing around, and you'd all agree to play a cash game in someone's garage or office until two or three in the morning when someone's wife would call to see if he was in a ditch.

The real trouble began when one of my friends moved into an apartment over the downtown bakery because his marriage fell apart. With no family or neighbors to disturb, he started hosting games several times a week. His old friends played as much as we could because well, we loved him as much as we loved to gamble, but the tenor of the games started to shift. More and more guys were showing up, driving in from other towns with wads of cash, betting hands so big you had to take greater risks just to compete.

Gambling, for me, was never about money. Sure, it was nice to go home with more money than you left with, and it hurt for a few days if you lost more than you could afford. However, it was more than winning or losing the night. It was always about being in the hand, in the magical moment of promise and suspense. If you never folded, gave up, walked away, and there was one more card to be played, you always had a chance.

🐇 🐇 🐇

I carry the heavy super out to my truck bed. A few stragglers have followed and are floating around the truck, settling on top of the screen. Most of them will make it home with me. I've hauled a swarm over sixty miles with stray bees clinging to the outside of a super, and they made the trip intact. Without a community, bees die. The animal kingdom is full of examples of the lone wolf, but I don't know of any stories of solitary insects. Bees don't just need a partner or a few friends; they need a colony. It's easy to get sentimental, in the midst of a bee removal, but even if I maintain this hive for years, it won't house the same bees I've been tussling with today. The queen lays thousands of eggs daily, and while the beekeeper doesn't notice it, the hive is constantly regenerating. The queen may live for several years, but her attendants work themselves to death within a matter of weeks.

It's important to remind myself of this because of what I'm about to do next: hauling the shop vac into the Sunday School room. The rescue portion of the day is complete. This is now an extermination job.

As power equipment goes, the shop vac has got to be the most obnoxious thing I own. When I flip the switch, the racket is maddening, but I'm not worried about being attacked because as soon as a bee zooms toward me, I whisk her out of the air. I don't believe my wet/dry vac is rated for honey, so I hold the nozzle a few inches above the remaining mess on the floor and in the walls and let the suction pull the bees to a quick death. Then I swipe around the windowsills until most of the bees are gone.

The worst of the task behind me, I turn to my Mason jars. The honey on the ground, trampled and mixed with wood shavings, mud, and dead bees is, of course, a total loss. There's enough heavy comb, however, wedged in the wall. Most honey you buy at the grocery store or farmer's market has been strained with perhaps a wedge of decorative comb sunk to the jar's bottom. The sweet cocktail I'm making, however, is a "dirty batch." I'm using the jar itself as a spoon, scooping up as much comb and honey as I can cram into the container. These walls aren't insulated, but

THE RISK INVOLVED

I do wonder what other residue I might be collecting. Ultimately, I may decide my harvest inedible, but after as much disruption and destruction I have visited on these bees, it seems sinful to walk away without honey.

If you are playing cards with a large stack of chips in front of you—chips you have mostly won from other players (rather than chips you've bought), then you are playing with "house money." Even if the honey I have collected is dirty and may need to be discarded, and the bees in the back of my truck may decide they dislike my backyard and flee, I have been playing with house money all day.

There comes a time, early morning, near the end of most poker games when it's evident you are not dragging yourself home as the big winner. Long ago, a country sage warned gamblers to never count their money while they're still at the table, and while this is probably wise advice, I suspect most players, myself included, do a quick estimate of their chip total as a game winds down. If it looks like you're more or less breaking even, then you're likely to slow play the remaining hands. If, however, you've rebought several times and you're fifty, sixty dollars in the hole, you're likely to go full tilt—play with reckless abandon, trying to win it all back in a few hands. You'll do things like bet hard on the hammer. Re-raise in an attempt to get everyone else to fold. Master the art of the bluff. And by "you" and "likely," I mean "me" and "absolutely." Full tilt rarely works, and I almost always went home empty-handed, but there's not much difference in degrees of regret between losing forty dollars or eighty.

Losing three hundred and fifty dollars in one evening, however, is a different story.

A buddy and I had both gotten knocked out of the river shed tournament by ten o'clock, and he knew about a cash game the next town over. I was low on funds, but I'd recently taken a job out of town, was playing less cards, spending less time with my friends. I agreed we should go all in on the night.

About thirty minutes later, we arrived at a dark house. No telltale signs—lights blazing, guys taking smoke breaks on the front porch—of a raucous poker game.

"You sure this is it?" I asked.

"It's around back," my friend said, stuffing a roll of cash into my hands.

"What's this?" I asked.

"Kind of a high-stakes game," he said. "Bet big to win big."

"Lose early. Win late," I said.

"Play smart," he said.

"You play smart."

A guy immediately met us at the door of an enclosed carport. He'd been watching us on a security camera monitor mounted on the wall behind him. Eight players were seated around the table, but it was a pretty quiet room. Not the constant trash talking that accompanies games where everyone knows one another. At first, I thought the security cameras were there because there was so much money passing hands, but the main reason was because the food and beer were free. And the food and beer were free because this was a game where the house took a rake—a percentage of the winnings—from every pot. In theory, this is all fine—it's the way many casinos operate. In reality, however, for private games in Texas, it happens to be illegal.

By this time in my gambling life, I had spent hundreds of hours playing thousands of hands of Hold 'Em; I could glance at my hole cards, compare them to the flop, and know in an instant where I stood; I knew a pair of kings were "cowboys," and two jacks were a "pair of hooks;" knew about raises and re-raises, position and bullshit bets, when to hold 'em, when to fold 'em, and when to bluff. I also knew about gorillas—noisy guys who just keep calling and raising every bet, trying to knock others out of the game, but I had never played with a guy who rebought a hundred dollars' worth of chips every thirty minutes. The classic gorilla is usually in cahoots with someone else at the table.

THE RISK INVOLVED

The gorilla makes all the noise and flashy bets to fatten the pot while his partner quietly wins the majority of hands. I was never able to identify who his partner might be, but I knew one thing for certain: it wasn't me.

Around every poker table, there's a mark—a player who doesn't really know what he's doing, either because of inexperience, he's been drinking too much, or he has a "tell," which is an unconscious tic that reveals if he's hit his hand or is bluffing. And every gambler knows, if you can't identify the mark at the table, then it's you.

All I know is after three free beers and several hours, my buddy and I were flat broke, weaving our way out the door and back to his car.

"Well, that sucked," I said.

"Just. Not. Our. Night."

"Been too long," I said. "You and me being stupid like this."

"I've missed it," he said.

"Me too."

We drove in silence the rest of the way back to town.

"You can pay me back Monday," my friend said, as we pulled in front of my house.

I nodded. Thanked him for the ride.

"We should do this more often," he said.

"We should," I agreed.

Before I even made it to the front door, fumbling for my keys, however, I knew it would be a long time before I ever played cards again.

On my way home, truck full of bees, I call the church president one last time.

"I've done what I could," I tell him.

"What do I owe you?" he asks.

"Oh, I should pay you," I say. "I haven't had this much fun in a long time."

"Well, we'll figure something out," he says. I assure him I'll return tomorrow to see if there are any remaining bees and remind him I've destroyed a good portion of the wall and carpet. My truck cab reeks of sweat and burnt wood, but I decide not to mention that the Sunday School room probably also has smoke damage.

Three gnarled cedar trees grow in a cluster in the back corner of our yard near a yucca plant, crepe myrtle, and tall weeds. Shortly after we moved here, I built a raised platform around the tree trunks. I added steps with a simple archway, and my daughters enjoyed endless tea parties in their treehouse. After my son was born, I added a tower on the side with a hinged wall for a secret entrance, even though he enjoyed tea parties more than swashbuckling. It's been a while since any of my children have enjoyed an afternoon of high tea, so I decide I'll turn the space into my apiary.

The secret doorway is about four feet high, but once inside, I can stand up straight. A quick measurement indicates the hive boxes will all fit with just enough space for me to maneuver around three sides. I lay a cinderblock base to provide elevation in wet weather, and to discourage fire ants during dry weather. Box hives were uniquely designed to house honeybees, but unfortunately, they also provide an ideal source of food and water for other insects. Once the bottom board is in place, I rest the full bee box on top, rip off the screen from the top and entrance, carefully place an empty shallow super with frames on top, cover it with the telescoping lid, and slip out of the Sunday School bees' new home.

The bees have been too stunned to pay me any mind; however, once they notice me, they will be eager to drive me away. I pause a few minutes, peering over the tower. Bees spill from the mouth of the hive and crawl along the ledge, picking up the scent of previous residents. A few float up and cling to sides of the tower, momentarily, before rising to the top and setting off to scout for pollen and water. My beekeeping adventures for the day are finished, and soon I'll wash off the sticky honey, the stench of smoke, perhaps return to grading papers, but more than likely, I'll prepare for classes by reading a novel or poems. For the bees, there are no days of rest. Inside the hive, I imagine they are already separating their dead from the honey where they'll be pushed over the side. They are investigating the shallow super's frames, pulling wax to form into comb. They are sealing cracks with propolis. They are tending to the queen and the brood. There's a 50/50 chance that they'll still be here in the morning. Or they'll find something unsatisfactory about this space and relocate in a hollow branch or a neighbor's garage. A chance that my morning labors and their afternoon work will have all been in vain. As much as I am eager for them to stay and will be disappointed if they go, I won't regret the day at all; the thrill of working with bees, win or lose, is always worth the gamble.

WHITE PICKET FENCES

In this town, you practically have to die in your home before people accept you really lived here. For fifteen years, my wife and I have called the house on the corner of San Jacinto and Plum Street home; we've raised three children here, made one hundred and seventy nine mortgage payments, paid taxes and insurance, had the roof replaced, raked leaves, cut the grass, planted flowers, vegetables, and the occasional fruit tree, buried two dogs, three cats, a hermit crab, and countless chickens in the backyard, and people still ask, *you live in the Schmidt house, don't you?* Our last name is not Schmidt.

In fairness, the Schmidt family is legendary in Central Texas. As one of the first families of Texas barbecue, they've been smoking meat since the 1940s, and they own two of the four meat markets in town. *Texas Monthly's* best barbecue in the state consistently lists fare from a Schmidt family pit. I didn't realize the scope of their notoriety, however, until a few months after I started a business in town, and a middle-aged man rushed into my office.

"What's the best place in town to get barbecue?" he asked.

"You looking for brisket, pork ribs, or sausage?" I asked. By that time, I had eaten at all four places numerous times and learned that locals are required to have a definitive opinion on which pits produced the best types of meat.

"I don't know." He pointed to an enormous RV parked out front. "We drove down here from Minnesota."

"For barbecue?"

"Seeing some friends and family throughout the South but came here especially for meat."

"From Minnesota?" I asked.

"Oh, this town is all over the food channels," he said, smiling. "I've been thinking about smoked meats for days."

Several months after we moved in, the widowed Mrs. Schmidt, ninety-years-old, returned to the neighborhood to visit friends, one of whom brought her to meet us. As the matriarch shuffled quietly through our home, I felt proud because we had spiffed things up a bit, painted all the walls a variety of vibrant colors, ripped out ancient carpet to reveal hardwood floors, and removed dark shades to flood rooms with sunlight. The only thing I recall her saying during this short visit, however, is: *what have you done to my house?*

So, yes, call it what you will: we live in the house that barbecue built.

The backyard, roughly a quarter of an acre, is enclosed with a white picket fence that, when we bought the place, was in dire need of repair. Neighbors warned us, however, that we could never tear it down, we were to host the annual National Night Out gathering, and that Mrs. Schmidt had left boxes of garland, bows, and Christmas lights in the shed. We moved in mid-December, and I have never neglected to trim the fence.

One afternoon, not long after we'd settled in, I came home for lunch to see an older gentleman repairing the gate that separates my backyard from our closet neighbor. The barrier isn't what you'd call a shared fence; it's a good ten feet back from the property line on my side of the yard. I introduced myself to the gate-repairer and asked how his work was progressing.

"Your neighbor said the gate was sticking," he said. "No idea how many times I've shored this up."

"Well," I said. "I appreciate it."

"Nice to meet you," he said.

"Same."

A few days later, our neighbor presented us with the bill, told us there was no hurry to pay her back. She figured we didn't know any good handymen in town yet, and she'd been having such a problem with the gate. I was too flummoxed in the moment to ask why she needed unfettered access to my property, and it wasn't until several weeks later that I gained a better understanding of the community we had joined. We returned from a weekend out of town to find a bag of homegrown green beans on our kitchen table, a nice gesture except we had not left a house key with anyone. A few days later, our neighbor asked if we enjoyed the beans.

"Yes," I said. "But how did they get in our house?"

"I've had a key to that house for years," she said. "Not giving it up because somebody new lives here."

This did not sit well with me, but I kept silent, and that silence grew into a grudging acceptance that, as the years passed, has grown into me not giving a second thought to having six extra keys made—one for all the neighbors—when we replaced our front door.

Over time, I have also replaced all thirty-four fence posts, and six-hundred-seventy-one rotting pickets. I've rebuilt three gates. And painted, repainted, and painted again the fence, trying to maintain the whiteness of the white.

This is a nice neighborhood, the real estate agent told us when we were looking for houses. *Nice neighbors.* And, if you swung by our backyard with a six-pack and a few links of sausage for National Night Out, you'd meet two retired pastors, a couple who owns the oldest pharmacy in town, two school administrators, a librarian, math teacher, two kindergarten teachers, a couple who own a car dealership, and a dentist who also happens to be the mayor. Finally, of course, you'd meet the giver-of-green-beans. She is a widow of many years who runs an alterations business out of her house. All hours of the day, a steady stream of people come and go with clothes that need mending and gossip to share. She is our very own town crier.

Once you've met my neighbors and had your fill of barbecue, beer, and gossip, make sure you note how lush and manicured everyone's lawn is, the neatness of bushes, absence of peeling paint, and the newness of roofs. The sidewalks that line everyone's lawns and the well-maintained streets that run by our houses. You might also notice how many amenities are within walking distance: multiple churches, the largest grocery store in town, the post office, the historic square with banks, insurance and title companies, restaurants, and shops. Even the fire station is nearby, which means emergency vehicles can reach our homes within minutes. The police station, however, is miles away, south of downtown, which is fine: this is a safe neighborhood. Safe and nice, full of good people (they all have keys to my home, for heaven's sake). You might also notice, as you look back to wave one last time, that all my neighbors, to a person, are white. As white as me, my wife, and our three children.

The schools in the neighborhood are good is something else the real estate agent told us as we first toured the house. I didn't give schools, good or otherwise, much thought because none of our children were school age at the time. However, one afternoon, I was in my office when an acquaintance popped his head in my door. He'd moved here only a few months before I did and was having about as much luck trying to sell subprime mortgages from his kitchen as I was having trying to sell insurance from an office on the historic square. We met because we both found ourselves spending time and money at the same advertising-mixer-volunteer opportunities where we discovered that everybody in town knows everybody else in town and have been doing business with somebody else long before we moved to town.

"You want to go see the Black high school?" he asked.

"I think there's only one high school here," I said. "A few blocks from my house."

"No," he insisted. "The Black school is abandoned. Other side of town."

I was probably making cold calls to drum up business, an activity I detested, so I was grateful for the distraction even though I understood that the *other side of town* meant the part of town where white people, like him and me, don't live.

According to the historical marker on the Black high school property, the building was constructed in 1923 with "materials salvaged" from another school. The Black high school, a formidable stucco structure, however, remained in use until 1964 when the school district finally fully integrated.

The mortgage broker and I poked around the overgrown perimeter of the building, watching for snakes. Plywood covered most of the windows and doors, and my acquaintance said he'd heard the attic was infested with bats. He talked about investment property, how all someone would need to do is pay back taxes, turn the space into chic apartments or horse stables. I didn't have enough cash to invest in my own business so half-listened to his schemes. Besides, I had a sense we were definitely trespassing. This field trip, however, got me thinking again about schools, about the fact that the schools in my neighborhood are "good." The fact is, three of the four elementary schools, along with the only junior high and high school in town are all within walking distance from my house.

"Good schools," "nice neighbors," and "safe neighborhoods" are all phrases white people use with other white people to demarcate the white boundaries of their cities and towns. And our town, like many in the United States, is divided by a major highway and railroad tracks. The eastside is predominately a Hispanic community, while white neighborhoods fan out west of downtown, and north of the tracks is where Black folks mainly call home. These demographic lines have blurred, even in the fifteen years I have lived here, and there are newer, more diverse subdivisions scattered throughout the county; however, I suspect that nonwhite residents, especially if they are first- or second-generation inhabitants of this town can clearly show me how every street, store, school, park, and church is marked. The "white" may be implied, but it is never silent.

The one school not in my neighborhood is George Washington Carver, which houses all the kindergarten children in the county. The campus sits in close proximity to the abandoned Black high school and borrowed its name from the high school when it was shuttered. I am unsure when the school district made the decision to send all children to one kindergarten, but I suspect it was after most of the town's older white folks' children had advanced to first grade. The assumption might be unfounded, but I really started thinking about the town's demographics when my oldest child attended Carver, and I started eating lunch in the cafeteria once a month.

If you have never eaten lunch in a school overcrowded with five- and six-year-olds, the decibel level is akin to a heavy metal concert. I was also unprepared for how the noise and frenetic movement of little people crowded into one space (where is the fire marshal?) brought back waves of school-related childhood anxiety. The first time I ate in my daughter's cafeteria, I was so distracted that I spent most of the time watching the cafeteria clock, willing the minutes to pass. *Only seven more.* By the second time I ate lunch with her, however, I was more acclimated and had the opportunity to look around the room, to really see the other children. Other than my daughter, there were very few white kids. In my first four years of school back in Kentucky, there were no Black or brown kids, and so I was pleased my children would be growing up in a more diverse school system. Then another thought hit me: *where did all these children and their parents live?*

The thing I am most embarrassed by is that I did not move to this town specifically to live in white spaces. I delivered Meals on Wheels for both my church and for the Kiwanis Club, which meant during the lunch hour every May, I traveled routes through town that took me down almost every street. I was also selling insurance for years in town, and I had to take pictures of any house I insured, which meant I had travelled down nearly every road in the entire county. By the time I was sitting in the kindergarten cafeteria wondering where all these Black and brown children lived, I had more than likely passed by their homes at some point or another.

There is a difference between seeing and knowing. I knew the county was minority/majority, but the circles I spent most of my time in were white. I saw that the majority of my clients were nonwhite, saw that the majority of my daughter's classmates were nonwhite but chose not to know what that said about the dearth of nonwhite people in my own neighborhood.

The largest small-town parade I've ever witnessed lines up the second Saturday of every June in my neighborhood. My children and I walk the streets that surround our house and watch as the Chamber of Commerce queens and kings from seemingly every county in Texas don their elaborate costumes while parents reattach floral arrangements to floats, and local businesses, trying to outdo one another, put the finishing touches on landscapes constructed in the back of pickup trucks and hay trailers. The cheer squad usually ends up behind our backyard, and we

THE RISK INVOLVED

listen to shrieks, popping balloons, and *we've got spirit, yes we do* for an hour or so before the parade begins. Eventually, we weave our way near the center of town to watch the parade in motion.

A few years back, we found ourselves on the courthouse lawn, and as I tried to position myself for a better view, I noticed I was standing next to a monument dedicated to the memory of the men from this county who fought and died for the Confederacy during the American Civil War.

Confederate monuments, battlegrounds, and legends of the South are as intertwined with my childhood memories as are fishing, hog killings, and sad country songs. I was born in the northernmost tip of Kentucky, as close to being a Yankee without being one by the Grace of God and geography (as my father would say). Growing up, the Civil War seemed a fairy tale, fought on both sides by well-meaning people, protecting their way of life. Abraham Lincoln, Kentuckian by birth, shepherded us through our flawed way of thinking, paid the martyr's price, and set us back on the path of liberty and justice for all. I lost interest in American history shortly after the moment Robert E. Lee hauled himself up the steps of the Appomattox Courthouse, and Lincoln's body wended its way as "lilacs last in the dooryard bloom'd."

This past summer, though, a petition circulated through town, demanding that the Civil War monument be removed. The stone memorial was erected in 1920, probably gifted to the county by the daughters of the Confederacy, probably in the spirit of maintaining the norms of segregation as much as honoring dead farm boys.

County officials voted to remove the monument but didn't have the funds to execute the project. Talk circulated about installing a plaque with more historical context. Some folks suggested relocating the monument to the county museum. I suspect that a few residents hoped the symbolic vote for removal would suffice until all the controversy blew over. Nobody seemed to know what to do with a hunk of granite emblazoned with a Confederate flag.

JEFFREY UTZINGER

On the way home from picking up lumber for a greenhouse I was building, I received a call from a county commissioner who calls me every couple of years to ask if I can help him remove bees from sheds or a tree stump on his land.

"I was wondering if you'd serve on a committee to decide what to with the monument," he said.

Oh, why can't you be calling about bees?

"Of course," I said.

A few weeks later, nine of us gathered in the upper chambers of the county courthouse: eight older white men, one Black woman, and one Black man. I have sung hymns with most of the people at community-wide worship services over the years, done business with a few, served on various committees with most, hiked in Big Ben National Park with two of them, and count one gentleman as a mentor and close friend. However, the start of the meeting felt like a gathering of strangers, a high-stakes poker game where nobody is good at reading anyone else's face.

The organizer suggested we go around the circle one-by-one and share our thoughts on what to do with the monument. He volunteered to start. If you were to search the internet for images of a "Texan," the organizer's picture, or a close approximation, would appear—a white man with a big grin, a gray moustache, close-cropped hair that is covered with a cowboy hat (when he's not indoors). I like this guy but was dreading what he was about to say. However, he set a pattern for what almost every white guy there said: a fascination with the Civil War, usually the result of a father's or grandfather's influence, a recounting of the books we'd read, the movies that shaped our childhoods, an acknowledgment that slavery was evil, and a nearly unshakable belief that monuments dedicated to the Confederacy were in honor of hard scrabble, country boys—boys very similar to what we imagined ourselves to have once been—and not markers celebrating racism.

THE RISK INVOLVED

"But this summer," he said, "after talking to folks, I've come to the conclusion that the monument is hurtful to the Black folks in town. It needs to come down."

I could have hugged him. I recounted my very similar journey, followed by others in the group.

Mrs. B., the only female among us, mainly talked about Jesus, about bringing people together, about ways to tell more stories about the Black people of our community.

I was feeling enlightened. That we were working toward being on the right side of history. And then, Ron, the last person in the circle, the only Black man among us, began to talk. Everybody in town, no matter where you live, knows Ron. He owns a landscaping business and has served on the Commissioners Court since I moved to town. I don't know that anyone has ever bothered to run against him. He has a low, soft voice and a gentle demeanor. If you searched the internet for images of "a really nice guy," I think you'd find a picture of Ron.

Ron, however, made no reference to the American Civil War, no national narratives with which he'd had to come to grips. No talk of Jesus.

"When I was a kid," Ron started, "my friends called me 'unconcerned.' I wasn't really sure what it meant, but I guess it's because I'm easygoing. Never wanted to cause trouble. Didn't like fights."

He told us a story about the first professional level job he'd had at a chemical plant where he was in charge of checking samples for purity. There was a white guy, Ron told us, who wasn't very good at his job, and Ron kept sending back his samples. One day, the guy called the front office, didn't know he was talking to Ron, and said *somebody needs to tell that Black fellow he better watch himself.*

But Ron didn't say "Black fellow"; he dropped the racial slur with a hard R and sat for a moment to let it echo around the spacious courthouse room.

It dislodged a world of childhood memories of growing up in Kentucky: if someone has a bowl of mixed nuts in a crystal bowl around Christmastime, I think of the word because a relative used it in conjunction with "toes" when describing Brazil nuts. It's what white folks in my youth called the hired men who helped bring in hay every fall. It's the word whispered when describing which parts of the county one was best to avoid. It's a word my cousins and I would bandy about when we wanted to shock each other with jokes we'd learned while eavesdropping on adults. I've heard echoes of the word behind family members' concerns about what the world has become.

Nobody that I know uses the word in polite company, not even in conspiratorial whispers anymore. When Ron said it, I couldn't even recall the last time I'd heard it from a live human voice. Something shifted in the room. It was like someone had fired a pistol, and we were all waiting for our hearing to recover.

That Ron, a Black man, dropped it causally in a story, in a setting that we all knew was largely performative, when we were about county business and that these conversations were likely to be repeated, suggested that it was a word he had heard spoken aloud many times in his presence and, more than likely, not in the so distant past.

Of all the stories he could have told, I wondered why he told that one. I've come to the conclusion that it was a story crafted to make white people uncomfortable but not too uncomfortable—it was, after all, a story set a long time ago in another town. No one in that room, or even anyone who was related to anyone in that room, had called him that name. *Relax* I read in his eyes. *I know y'all are nice people who live in good neighborhoods.*

He ended with this: "So my entire life, I have gone along to get along. I've been unconcerned but no more. I want to say clearly today that the monument has got to go. Don't care how or where or who pays. It just needs to go."

Hell, I thought. *Why didn't Ron speak first?*

THE RISK INVOLVED

This summer, I've been working on a building project that requires around four hundred glass bottles, and while I am committed to drinking as much as possible and still maintaining a reputation in my good neighborhood, there's really only so much one man can do. There is a recycling center on the edge of town where, a few years ago, I could have raided barrels over the span of two weekends and collected all the bottles I needed. Apparently, however, open recycling centers are an invitation for people to abandon their used motor oil and unwanted couches, and so when I went to visit, I found the center enclosed in a locked, chain-link fence. I went a few days later during the posted operating hours, and a friendly city employee told me that I could only drop off recyclables. Scrounging was no longer permitted.

"You should try the back alleys behind the bars," he said.

It was a good idea, and one I considered as I drove away, but then I remembered the lot behind one of the barbecue restaurants. They have several dumpsters and often stack empty bottles next to piles of firewood. I knew this because the pitmaster's brother and I used to be in Kiwanis together, and the club stored American flags in one of the storage spaces attached to the back of the restaurant. We raised money by planting flags in people's yards on patriotic holidays, and if it was your holiday to make the flag run, then you spent time in the morning and the afternoon loading and unloading flags in the lot.

I parked on the side street, donned my rubber gloves, and pulled a cardboard box from my trunk. No crates of empty glass were visible, so I walked a little farther toward the building to see if there were any bottles closer to the back doors. It was near dusk, and I was trespassing on private property, wearing gloves and carrying a box, and I realized that if you searched the internet for images of "white privilege," you might find a picture of me.

JEFFREY UTZINGER

When I first heard the phrase "white privilege," I thought it meant rich white people. It didn't mean people whose maternal grandfathers drank themselves to death, people whose uncles taught them how to plant tobacco and bale hay, or people whose fathers spent their early years in foster homes, or people who wore their cousin's hand-me-downs until they were in high school. No, my people grew up poor, worked hard for what they got, clawed their way to the middle class. If I knew any privileged white people as a kid, it was only because my family and relations worked for them.

Years ago, when I worked at a chemical plant in south Austin, I became close with a guy named Henry. He worked directly with the chemicals, and I worked maintenance, but the plant was small, so you ran into everybody several times a day. My main job was to paint and repaint everything in the plant, which was good job security because the chemicals corroded everything quickly. I also washed out drums and crushed the metal ones with a fork lift, so they could be hauled away. And since I was just a part-timer (college kid, passing through to something bigger) without a real job description, I also did whatever any of the guys needed me to do. Henry was the first person to ever engage me in a serious conversation about race. Oh, I had studied race, written about race, been involved in long academic conversations about race but only in classrooms taught by white teachers and professors, surrounded by white classmates.

Henry quietly showed me the difference between seeing and knowing.

Since the working conditions at the plant were so hazardous, the company bought us leather safety boots to wear, and the chemicals ate through the soles so quickly that we had to replace our boots every six months or so. They almost seemed disposal to me, but I noticed that at the end of every day, while everyone was changing into their street clothes, Henry sat and polished his boots.

"Why do you keep them so nice when they're going to wear out?" I asked. "They buy us new ones."

He laughed and kept brushing. I thought he was ignoring me because he didn't say anything else. We both dressed and walked out to the parking lot at the same time. When we got close to my truck, he finally spoke.

"You ever notice that white people don't keep their cars clean?"

"Guilty," I said. In high school, after my parents had bought me my first car, my mother came in my room one afternoon and asked me if I would go wash my car because it was driving my father crazy that I wasn't fussing over it more. Every vehicle I've ever owned is grimy inside and out.

"Dirty cars and dirty shoes," Henry said.

"Oh," I said. It was my turn to laugh. "Never thought there was a connection."

"You've never had to think about it," he said.

I don't recall when I finally made the "connection," but it's been a good twenty-plus years since Henry pointed it out to me. I have the privilege of driving a dirty car, of trucking around with scuffed shoes, of running late to meetings, of half-assing a job now and then, of drinking too much in public, of moving through my day, self-absorbed, blissfully unaware of my surroundings because nobody is judging me. That's not entirely true—of course, people are judging me, every day. I just have the privilege of ignoring it. Of not caring. Of going through my entire day without ever thinking: "my shoes are dirty" or "my car needs a wash" or "my skin is white."

JEFFREY UTZINGER

Trespassing behind a business in ridiculous garb, looking for bottles that you can incorporate into a greenhouse without expectation or fear that the owner will pop out the back door or that a police cruiser will pass by is the very definition of privilege. Because you know that if either of these things occur, all you have to say is: *Hey, I'm just a middle-aged white guy. I live in a nice neighborhood where the schools are good. Yeah, the Schmidt house on the corner, the one with the white, picket fence.*

COUNT YOUR CHICKENS

On Good Friday, I brought home a cardboard box full of six baby chicks. My wife used a large serving spoon as a silent baton to indicate the box needed to be removed from the dining room table. She then resumed polishing silver in preparation for the hoard of guests who would be descending on our home for Easter weekend. I had been picking up last-minute items, and live chickens were not on my list. However, my chance to recreate a special childhood memory for our three young children—baby chicks for Easter!—was slipping away. Our oldest daughter was nearly a teenager, and her brother and sister were not far behind. They rushed into the dining room when I called, and I handed them the box, told them to grab a roll of paper towels and set the chicks loose in the sunroom. My mother-in-law emerged from the kitchen, wiping her hands on her apron with a look that said *after twenty-five years, this is exactly the type of behavior I've come to expect.*

"Where are you going to put them?" Christa asked.

"I'll build a coop in the backyard," I said.

"I mean now," she said. "Tonight. This weekend?"

To ease her misgivings, I told her about the additional purchases still in the truck: a fifty gallon, galvanized watering tank for temporary

THE RISK INVOLVED

chicken housing, a bale of shaved wood chips, a bag of starter feed, and a heat lamp. I even remembered plastic hanging containers for food and water.

"Did you remember the tables for Sunday?" she asked.

I had.

That night, we participated in "the stations of the cross," a prayer and meditation service that dates back to the thirteenth century; St. Francis of Assisi wanted to simulate the Via Dolorosa—the sorrowful road—that Jesus traveled on the way to his crucifixion. Each of the fourteen stations are designed to encourage participants to contemplate suffering and death. It's an admittedly weird thing to do, but the Year of the Chicken Surprise, I was seeking meaning in life more than usual because I was convinced that I was going to die. Not in the long, slow way we understand that someday all of this will end, but in the come-to-Jesus-I'm-going-to-die-within-the-next-few-weeks, terrifying way. During the previous six months, I'd been having frequent bouts of severe vertigo accompanied with involuntary rapid eye movement, extreme nausea, and vomiting.

The most distressing part was that puking to the point of dry heaves did not provide relief in the way that purging after food or alcohol poisoning often does. After the retching ceased, I would began to shiver because my clothes, down to my socks and underwear, were soaked with sweat. The fits lasted for three to four hours, and the only tenable position was to lie flat and motionless as though someone had nailed my entire body to the floor.

Episode One: A group of my friends meets every Thursday for a men's book group, and one morning, our host insists we take a shot of homemade Hungarian Schnapps he's recently acquired on a trip abroad. A low buzz sounds in both my ears, and the space between my shoulder blades tightens as I down my drink. I cannot exactly locate the rungs of the stool on which I am seated, and so I slip away to the bathroom where the barfing, the chills, the sweat, and the stretching out immobile commences. A few hours later, my friend summons his father-in-law, a retired doctor, and the two of them pry me off the floor, ease me into a car, and manage to take me home.

Had the alcohol alone caused these sensations, I might have been intrigued, but this was not my first taste of hard liquor. It was also not my first bout with vertigo. In retrospect, I've identified it as "Episode One" because it was the worst fit I'd had in years, and it was the first in a string that repeated itself two days later, then several times the following week, the following month, and so on.

Episode Two: sitting at the kitchen table, trying to learn a baffling new method of long division in a fruitless attempt to help my son with homework, I look toward the microwave clock, and the kitchen shifts. Using walls and furniture to balance, I lurch my way to the back bathroom, throw up until there is only bile, and then the dry heaves. Around dusk, I text Christa to bring me a blanket; I am shivering cold but unable to stand.

"I made a doctor's appointment," I tell Christa as she sits on the floor beside me.

"I think that's a good idea," she says.

Later, she would admit that my initiative to schedule a doctor's appointment scared her more than the actual unexplained dizziness and blowing of chunks.

After checking in at the doctor's office, I experienced a wave of anxiety, wondering what I would do if I got sick in the waiting room. Thus began a routine I followed each time I was in public: scoping out the availability of restrooms, exits, and end-of-aisle seating. Standing if there was any possibility of being trapped by nonfamily members. Leaving altogether if a room was too crowded. Checking symptoms— Are my ears ringing? Are my shoulder blade muscles tight? Did anyone else see that object move?—over and over and over again.

A medical assistant ran routine tests, asked me a series of questions, listened to my complaints. The family doctor slipped into the room, repeated most of the process, asked most of the same questions, studied notes on his laptop, and finally declared that I was an otherwise healthy man approaching middle age. He needed to refer me to a specialist in vertigo.

When I called the Ear, Nose, and Throat office, the receptionist told me the doctor was only in town on Tuesdays, and the next available appointment was several weeks away.

"I think I'm dying," I said. It was the first time I had said the words aloud.

"Probably not," the receptionist answered with cheerful condescension. I was raised by people who put the best construction on everything, and so a stranger denying the reality of my death in the near or distant future was an assurance I clung to as gospel.

I was also raised by people who were raised on farms; we come from a long line of folks who wrung chicken necks for Sunday dinner shortly after returning from a service of fervent prayer and hymns of praise. The idea of bringing home baby chickens at Easter would not have occurred to any of my ancestors unless said birds were going to provide deviled eggs or drum legs later in the year. My uncle ran a dairy farm, raised hogs, chickens, and sheep, and one of my favorite times of the year was chicken killing. After the thrill subsided of watching literal chickens running with their heads cut off, my uncle threw my cousins and me severed chicken claws that we would bind together with bailing twine to craft into make-believe grappling hooks.

So the Easter memory I was trying to fabricate for my children was not one I experienced but rather a childhood television memory in which children receive pastel pink or baby blue chicks to accompany their hollow chocolate Easter bunnies. In recent years, however, dyeing a chick to give to a child who grows bored with it once the chick becomes a pullet has been deemed cruel, and feed stores have ceased coloring birds. To further discourage the practice of giving chicks as pets, the minimum number you can now purchase is six. It's also a number that lends credence to the first moment you find yourself hitching your pants a little and telling people, *yeah, I got chickens. Whole flock.*

For the first few weeks, the chicks lived in my home office, safely enclosed in their trough filled with wood shavings, warmed by the glow of orange light. Somewhere in my stack of DIY books were plans for backyard coops, and Christa had located a whole world of chicken tiny houses online. However, after Easter dinner, I suggested a group of us take a walk around the neighborhood because I thought I'd seen something resembling a chicken coop among the menagerie of homemade wooden goods that a man down the street sells in his front lawn.

The bottom half of the two-story coop was a rectangle frame enclosed with chicken wire, on top of which sat the roosting area fashioned from scraps of cedar and roof shingles. The second floor was segmented into six laying boxes, each with its own door that opened to the outside for easy egg gathering. A wooden ladder served as a stairway between the floors, and overall, the coop looked like a cozy, little barn.

"It says two hundred dollars," the man hollered from his porch swing, "but I'll take one-fifty in cash if you'll haul it off today."

"Sounds fair," I said.

"Come around back. I'll give you a tour."

A massive chicken coop covered half his backyard. There were doors, latches, laying boxes, feeders, gates; a veritable amusement park for chickens or, at the very least, a retiree's paradise. At that moment, I could have nailed the interviewer's question: *where do you see yourself in five years?* The only troubling thing, however, was the lawn portion of his yard was scorched earth dirt, pecked clean of vegetation by his countless chickens. I envisioned eventually housing my own chickens in a rolling coop, so they could trim grass and weeds, keep insects in check, and fertilize the lawn as I strategically moved them every couple of weeks throughout the backyard. I was unaware that chickens eat grass to the roots and then eat the roots. That they attempt to devour anything growing in a garden. That they love shredding flowers. They are basically goats with wings. Nonetheless, I returned home for cash and my truck to haul my own starter coop home.

Within three weeks, however, all six chickens were dead.

By the time I got an appointment with the ENT, I experienced more debilitating episodes. Episode Three: driving home from work, I turn to look at something in the median, and the car seems to lift, to fly, but not in a pleasant dream sequence sort of way. Somehow, without sideswiping other vehicles or flipping into a ditch, I manage to white-knuckle the car into a church parking lot where I grind the transmission into park, fling open the door, and vomit.

If this were a different sort of story, the moment I careened my car into a church parking lot where I expelled the poison from my body at the foot of the cross would be the climax. The point of no return, signaling the start of my road to recovery. This is not that sort of story.

Everybody has their cross to bear is often delivered with an eye roll, a world-weary shorthand to explain somebody or something that everybody in the room agrees is a pain in the ass. Personal suffering, therefore, is not a thing most of us want to discuss, a condition we prefer to contemplate, manage, and try to understand in private. During the worst of my mysterious vertigo, I became a fatalist. Life is hard. Expect the worst. Be delighted each morning you wake. Everybody has their cross to bear.

"Everything looks normal," the ENT said after prodding my head and checking my chart. "Not sure what's going on."

What is it that you specialize in? I wanted to ask but didn't because he is a nice enough guy; he'd read the book I brought along and wanted to talk about literature. Besides, my ears have been fucked up for longer than he has been alive. I had so many ear infections as a small child that, in addition to tonsil removal, I had surgery to insert tubes in my eardrums on three occasions. The idea was that these temporary "ventilation tubes" drained excess fluid from the middle ear and would improve my hearing. All I remember is being mocked for the rubber ear molds I was required to wear while swimming so the tubes wouldn't wash out. I also understood, at a young age, that the human body is remarkable at recovery and regeneration, except when it comes to processing sound.

I couldn't understand why, if I was having difficulty making it through a day without toppling over into a pool of vomit, we were back to the mysteries of my faulty hammer, anvil, and stirrup.

"I'm sending you for a CT scan," he said.

"It sounds like there's always a chorus of crickets in my head," I said.

That's not helpful is not what he said, but the look on his face suggested as much.

Vertigo dominated my thoughts for weeks. I tracked how I slept, how I got out of bed, how I reached for books, and what I ate. I avoided bending over, turning my head, and sudden movements of any kind. I tried so hard to keep my head erect and my shoulders straight that my entire body was constantly tense. Every time I was pinned to a bathroom floor, I replayed the preceding minutes, and then hours, trying to locate what set the room spinning. It was like a prompt for a third-grade essay: what exactly did you see, feel, touch, taste, and hear that triggered this series of unfortunate events?

As a result of my intense focus on what was happening in the moment, I scheduled my CT exam with the diagnostic clinic without asking any big-picture-type questions. When I arrived for my appointment, I checked in, turned to find an empty chair in the waiting room, and while the room did not flip, my heart sank. Most of the patients were wearing baseball caps or scarves wrapped around their heads. *Oncology*, I remembered finally, *is the study and treatment of tumors.* Shit. *The ENT also thinks I'm dying.*

Since no one knows their actual expiration date, it's impossible to pinpoint the exact period of time when one should have a midlife crisis. Two years before the Year of Vertigo, however, at the age of forty-two, I walked away from running a small business, filed for bankruptcy, returned to teaching, and started pursuing a PhD in literature. Because the university where I teach is fifty miles from my home, and the university where I was doing graduate work is one hundred miles from my home, I was driving around seven hundred miles a week. I spent an unseemly amount of time at gas stations and eating fast food in my car. Late one evening, after a three-hour seminar discussing the difference between simulation and simulacrum, I was sipping gas station coffee and pumping gas when Christa called. She was sobbing.

"The chickens are dead."

"What? How?" I asked in what I hoped was a compassionate, rather than accusatory, tone.

"The dog clawed through," was all she could manage.

Christa (mercifully) buried the dead before I got home, so this was all I was able to piece together regarding the chicken massacre: the sun was shining, so the chicks had been moved from inside the house to enjoy their new coop. The other members of my family left the backyard for a few moments, during which time our dog, who has freakishly strong paws, allegedly ripped through the chicken wire. This is where the telling gets muddled.

"It looked like she just rolled around on them," Christa said.

"Like she was playing with them?" I asked.

"Maybe."

"She wasn't eating them?"

"There wasn't a mark on any of their bodies," she said. "I think their little hearts just stopped."

"I think a raccoon did it," our son said.

Even though the dog had retreated to another part of the yard when the family returned to the scene of the crime, there was no evidence a raccoon sauntered into our backyard in broad daylight, eluding the dog's notice, so it could rip into a chicken coop to play with baby chicks. That said, my family members are at their best when they refuse to believe something bad about another family member—even the dog. The best construction on everything.

"I'll be administering your IV," a nurse said when my name was finally called at the diagnostic clinic. With his scruffy beard and unkempt hair, he looked more like a mechanic than a medical professional, which I found oddly comforting. Being scanned for tumors is stressful. Bringing your car in because your brakes squeak? Not so much.

"An IV?" I asked.

He laughed.

"That a problem?" he asked.

"Needles in veins," I said. "I'll probably pass out."

For the second time that morning, my lack of curiosity regarding my medical condition was causing as much stress as the mystery condition itself. I could have asked the ENT why he was sending me for a scan, could have looked up the word "oncology" when I scheduled the appointment, could have called my sister-in-law, an honest-to-God oncologist, could have called my own sister to ask about CT scans because she has survived cancer and a massive heart attack and has more knowledge about medical procedures than any music teacher on earth. But I didn't. When Christa pressed me about my ENT visit, all I had said was *they want to run more tests*. I'm an educator; there are few words in my vocabulary more familiar than "test." Why ask follow-up questions?

The nurse checked my blood pressure, and I always have to study people's faces when they report the results to see if they look concerned because I have no idea what the numbers mean. The nurse smiled, so I assumed I passed the first test. Then he jabbed me with the needle, and I didn't faint. He rattled off a set of instructions about lying perfectly still once he conveyed me into the tube, about not moving my head, about shooting something into my veins midway through the scan. What he failed to mention was the wave of nausea that would overtake me when the liquid entered my body. I was so distracted trying to figure out how

I was going to throw up without moving my head that, by the time I worked myself into a real panic, the nausea passed, and my scan was complete.

A few days later when the clinic's name appeared on my phone, I let it go to voicemail. Wouldn't you want to know, immediately, if you were going to die? Not in the long, slow way we understand that someday all of this will end, but in the come-to-Jesus-I'm-going-to-die-within-the-next-few-weeks, terrifying way? Or wouldn't you want to know that your condition is chronic but not immediately fatal? Wouldn't you want to hear your statistical odds of survival based on treatment options, age, weight, and family history? I took a deep breath and stared out my office window that overlooks a nature preserve. Nothing but miles of trees and flittering birds. *For many a time, I have been half in love with easeful Death.* Chances are, at that moment, I didn't quote from Keats's devastatingly beautiful "Ode to a Nightingale." Nor is it likely that I reflected on the twelfth station of the cross in which Jesus cries *My God, my God, why have you forsaken me?* I have consumed forests full of poetry and scripture in hopes that one or the other, or both, would someday save me, but I find they rarely come to mind in the moment of crisis. I always need another tomorrow in order to reflect. I called the clinic.

"Your results came back negative," the nurse said. It is a wonder in this age of message crafting and endless surveys that the medical profession has never figured out the word "negative" means something bad in every single other walk of life. As she explained in careful medical jargon the details of my results, I wanted to interrupt to tell her I was studying to be a Doctor of Philosophy in literature, that I don't even know what blood pressure numbers mean.

"So, all of this is good?" I finally asked.

She laughed.

"Yes, I'm sorry," she said. "The results of your scan are normal."

My elation, however, was short-lived. All the results of the scan confirmed was that no one knew what in the hell was wrong with me.

Episode Four: there are six of us in a graduate seminar; I am seated at the midpoint of a semicircle, and we are moving around the horn sharing initial thoughts on Slavoj Žižek's *Welcome to the Desert of the Real*. My eyes start to flicker, and the muscles in my shoulders go into vice-grip mode. The girl next to me is smart but has a slight stutter and a tendency to ramble. I am determined not to leave the room (tilting) until I have stated unequivocally that we are not living in a simulation. Moments later, I am puking in the men's restroom at a large public university. Mercifully, it is late in the day, and for the next two hours as I sprawl next to the toilet in an enclosed stall, only one other person comes into the restroom. As time passes, however, I panic because I am not sure when the building is locked at night and if I'll be able to exit. At nine, when class ends, I stagger to collapse on the couches outside the classroom and wait. The rambling girl ambles over, nods, and hands me my laptop and book. The professor, tenured and not inclined to chitchat outside of class, is close behind. I heave myself off the couch to block his path.

"I have terrible vertigo," I say. "The doctors aren't sure what's wrong."

"Oh," he says, clasping his hands. "Like Jimmy Stewart in Hitchcock's film."

Fuck you, I want to say but do not.

Normally, the trip from the Language Arts building to the parking lot takes about ten to fifteen minutes. The walk to my vehicle this night is slow and circuitous. I steer clear of well-lit walkways in an effort to avoid people. Having walked drunk across a college campus on more than one occasion in my youth, I know how my gait appears. No desire, as a forty-year-old man, to explain to a security guard that I no longer have time to drink during the week. I work my way behind buildings, close to walls, so I won't topple over. Spend a few minutes on every bench and ledge I encounter. Forty-five minutes later, I make it to my car and drive the two-hour trip home with my head pressed against the headrest. Fortunately, the route is all country roads, and I know every curve and pothole well.

THE RISK INVOLVED

Still, I want to weep by the time I get home. I sleep on top of the covers, still clothed. Don't even hazard trying to remove my shoes.

I am eager to walk away from failing enterprises the moment my interest wanes; however, when something captures my imagination, I latch on until the bitter end. The spring after the demise of our first set of chicks, I talked Christa into going to the feed store with me to buy six new ones. The entire family was wary, but my rationale was we had managed to keep three children alive for over a decade; the chicken debacle was really the only blemish on our record. This time, we bought a ten-foot by ten-foot chain-link dog kennel we used to surround the vulnerable chicken coop. I cut away the mangled chicken wire from the coop and replaced it with a sturdier mesh. We zip-tied plastic netting around the bottom half of the kennel to keep small predators at bay. Finally, we covered the top of our chicken fortress with a porous tarp to discourage neighborhood cats (or the unlikely raccoon). We were three hundred dollars in before receiving even a single free egg.

That said, chickens really do make fabulous pets. Nearly every day after work, Christa and I would drag metal chairs into the dog kennel, share a beer, and dissect the day while chickens pecked our feet or vied for a seat in our laps. Their bodies are a beautiful light brown with a slightly darker neck and head feathers, which makes them look like they're wearing elegant collared dresses. One weekend, my youngest daughter and I painted the ends of the chickens' claws with nail polish, which, even though they pecked it off in a matter of days, gave them more personality than one might expect from a chicken. My son named them all, but he's the only one who can tell them apart. He's also the only one who can catch them when they flit over the fence, or when neighborhood kids want to see them up close. The boy is the Jesus-mother to our chickens.

For one brief moment in the Bible, Jesus adopts a female-gendered perspective, which also happens to invoke chicken imagery. Looking out over Jerusalem and bemoaning the city's propensity to stone prophets,

Jesus laments "how often I have longed to gather your children together, as a hen gathers her chicks under her wings, and you were not willing." I have never been wild about the theology of salvation through suffering; the idea of Jesus as a great mother hen, on the other hand, makes me happy every time I think about it.

As does this: in Thomas of Celano's *The Treatise on the Miracle of Saint Francis*, he asserts that St. Francis preached sermons to birds. After listening intently, "those little birds, rejoicing in wondrous fashion, according to their nature, began to stretch out their necks, to spread their wings, to open their beaks and to gaze on him." I don't preach to my chickens, but I do talk to them. They talk back. They are a happy bird.

"This breed lays oversized eggs," Christa informed me as she scrolled through chicken articles on her phone. While you can catalog order any fancy chicken you can imagine, our local feed store sells two main kinds: sexed (you're likely to get all females) or straight run (male and female mixed). Through searching images and chicken blogs, Christa determined our birds were, specifically, Buff Orpingtons.

"That's nice," I said.

"Oh no," she said.

"Oh no, what, oh no?"

"The eggs." She hesitated, pretending to read further into the article, but the information she needed to share, she already knew. "They can get stuck."

"Get stuck?" I asked. "In the chicken, get stuck?"

"It kills them sometimes," she said. "But there's a saltwater bath."

"We should take them back," I said.

"You massage the chicken." Christa made a circular rubbing motion as though I were unfamiliar with the mechanics of massaging a chicken, which in fairness to her, I was, but in fairness to me, the cure seemed beside the point.

"It's rare," she said. "For the egg to get stuck."

"One time," I said. "All it takes is one time."

THE RISK INVOLVED

The following day, I presented one of my coworkers who has raised chickens for years with this disturbing tidbit.

"You've got to get comfortable wringing a neck now and then," she said.

I winced and asked if she'd tried saltwater baths.

"Saltwater baths?" She practically snorted.

I met one of my eventual favorite students on her first day of college when she visited my office, announced she'd written a novel, and demanded I read it. She has cerebral palsy and compares her speech to a drunken slur, which, given my hearing loss, made for conversations that were often confusing, lengthy, and exhausting for us both. Nonetheless, we met weekly for three years to discuss the writing life.

"You need to read more good books," I'd say after reviewing each chapter.

"I need to live more," she'd say.

One afternoon, I told her that my vertigo had made me afraid to tie my shoes. That I'd considered calling her for advice several times because I couldn't figure out how to fasten them without bending over. In order to talk, she has to contort the muscles in her face, which often makes her look irritated, even when she is not. I have known her long enough, however, to discern when she actually is irritated.

"Anything an able-bodied person experiences that is temporary," she said, "is nothing like, not even close to, what it's like to be trapped in this body forever."

It was a reminder I needed.

Most religions contend suffering is one of the few things in this world that points us to the meaning of life. Christians argue that suffering produces endurance, endurance produces character, and character produces hope. Buddhists will tell you suffering is born of a desire for pleasure, things of the flesh, and longing for life eternal. Jews wrote the book on suffering, and despite what you've heard, the main point of Job is not patience. It's suffering. I could go on. Most choices I have made in life are predicated on seeking pleasure, avoiding pain, and if this were a different sort of story, my student's devastating admonishment would be the moment when I share with you lessons learned throughout my illness. This is not that sort of story.

"Given all your symptoms," the ENT said, "and the lack of any red flags from your scan, I think you have Meniere's Disease."

Even though I had never heard of this condition, I felt a wave of relief. I had something with a name. Diseases with names often have cures. And surely obscure diseases with no telethons, foundations, marches, or walks attached, must be so treatable as to be blasé. Hardly worth the designation of disease.

"We're really not sure what causes it," he said. "And there's not really a cure." Drastic measures, he went on to explain, involve something called a labyrinthectomy in which part of the inner ear is removed. It corrects the vertigo but takes your ability to hear along with it. In the long run, many people with Meniere's Disease lose all hearing in one or both ears.

"What should I do?" I asked.

"Don't search for it on the internet," he said. "People are just over-the-top not helpful."

"Not helpful," I repeated.

He did give me a brochure with ideas for exercise and diet to minimize the effects of vertigo. I remembered Mark Twain's fondness for his "nineteen injurious habits" as I read the list of things to avoid: caffeine, tobacco, alcohol, chocolate, salt, spicy food, and on and on.

I committed, however, to combating a miserable condition with a miserable regiment of self-denial. I am embarrassed to admit how much I missed ketchup.

Episode Five: Bending to retrieve a dry-erase marker, I stand to find my students tilting toward the walls. I dismiss class, stumble to my office, and throw up for several hours in my recycling bin.

THE RISK INVOLVED

Episode Six: Reaching for a glass on the top shelf, my shoulders tighten, and I feel off balance. I grab an ice pack and leave for work anyway. Midway there, I turn around for home where I will lie on my back all day, grading papers.

Episode Seven. Episode Eight. Episode Nine.

I started drinking again, eating potato chips, swilling coffee and ketchup. No need to heap temperance on top of an already bad situation. I saw a chiropractor, a massage therapist, joined a Meniere's support group online. The ENT was correct: over-the-top not helpful.

The tenth station of the cross focuses on Jesus being stripped of his clothing before he's nailed to a cross. Contemplating one's own nakedness in public is the stuff of nightmares for most of us, but the following year on Good Friday, as we moved through the meditations once again, this station is the one that spoke to me the loudest. Sure, I detest suffering, fear death, but I realized what scared me the most about my condition was the ever-present threat of humiliation.

Eventually the time between episodes grew longer; at first, months passed, and then an entire year. It's been nearly two years now, but occasionally the knot between my shoulder blades tightens, or I'll stand, feel off-balance, and the panic rises. Hearing aids have helped some with my auditory issues, but my hearing continues to deteriorate. When allergy season returns in fall and spring, the incessant cricket chirping sound in my head reaches near maddening levels. There are weeks when my left ear is useful only for keeping my reading glasses level. At times, such as at this very moment, I feel like I am underwater. I can see people's lips moving, but I comprehend little of what's being said. Sometimes I pretend to follow along by reading facial expressions. Sometimes I have to ask people to repeat themselves, reminding them of my hearing loss. The most frustrating part of an invisible condition, however, is that even people who know me well seem to forget on a daily basis. They face me and speak louder for a few hours and then, the next day, they try to engage me in conspiratorial whispers.

At times, I now completely understand the phrase stone deaf.

The final station of the cross is a meditation on Jesus being laid in a tomb because, as I've mentioned, Good Friday is about remembering suffering and death. Resurrection comes on Easter Sunday, and the reason eggs are associated with Easter is because they symbolize the promise of new life.

One of strangest parts of raising chickens in a suburban neighborhood is that after folks ask how many eggs we get each week, they ask about the rooster. I remind them that roosters aren't allowed in the city limits and can see a confused look, which indicates that I am about to have to explain the basics of sixth-grade sex education one more time.

"Hens lay eggs without a rooster," I say.

"Really?" Before they ask if my chickens are a special breed, I cut them off.

"Roosters fertilize eggs that turn into baby chicks," I say.

"Oh yeah," they usually say. "I guess I knew that."

We've bought eighteen chicks and two ducks over the past few years and gather four to five eggs each day to eat or give away. Since the original chicken debacle, we've had good luck keeping most of them alive. However, chicks are subjected to dehydration and cold in transport to feed stores, and we've lost two the first night we had them. With the most recent batch, I crept into my home office before sunrise, peered into the orange glow of the trough, and knew right away. Sleeping as a metaphor for death is so common as not to be interesting, and it's amazing how dissimilar the two things are in reality. Sleep looks similar to alert resting while death looks like complete surrender, no dreams fluttering behind closed lids. I picked up the dead chick and headed to the huge compost heap in my backyard where I've taken to burying our dead animals. The chick's body was still warm from being under the heat lamp, and even though I was certain she was dead, I couldn't bring myself to bury her in the leaves just yet. This isn't a resurrection sort of story; the dead chick remains eternally dead. However, I wanted to make

THE RISK INVOLVED

sure, so I stood by the compost heap for a full ten minutes cradling the little body and staring at the sky full of stars. Listening.

DUCK

    Walking through a near empty Wal-Mart, Saturday morning, carrying only a brand-new ax, it's difficult not to project the idea that *I am about to do an unspeakable thing.* And, I was. Had the lawn and garden checkout been open, then at least my fellow shoppers might have thought, *oh, he's run into a stubborn root.* But no, I had to lumber toward the front of the store, past the pharmacy, the inspirational books, and candy aisles to where automation has all but wiped out human cashiers, leaving me standing at a self-checkout station, unprepared for how odd it is to scan an ax. If I'm buying beer or permanent markers, the system locks down, and I'm forced to wait for manager approval. However, unvetted and unaided, I am apparently able to purchase a lethal tool. No one there with whom to exchange small talk, joking about whether I need a flimsy plastic bag to tote my ax home. It was just me, my new weapon, and a deep sense of dread.
    I'll spare you the details of the moment I lopped off the duck's head and take you, instead, back to the beginning of my days keeping poultry.
    My wife and I have raised a dozen or so chickens for several years now, enjoying their company, eating their eggs. The average lifespan of a yard hen is seven years, though we've lost a few to hundred-degree

weather. Last spring, we had ice and snow, and even though temperatures hovered around zero for a week, the chickens all survived. A fox roams the neighborhood occasionally, but we've never spotted it near our henhouse. Hawks and owls perch in nearby trees from time to time, but none have ever swooped in to carry away one of our feathered friends. And, despite a mishap with our first set of baby chicks and the family dog, we've been pretty lucky raising birds. All this to say, we don't cull the flock when someone stops laying. When our chickens are ready to die, they do so on their own terms.

The chickens had fared so well that I decided we also needed ducks.

I should explain that even though we have a fairly large yard, we live inside the city limits, so space and ordinances limit the amount and type of farm animals we raise. What I'd really like, in addition to chickens and ducks, are a few goats and rabbits. And a donkey. If you don't understand why I'd like a donkey, I doubt there's anything I can tell you to make you understand. I bristle when people claim, *there are two types of people in this world* because no proclivities in this world are reducible to neat dyads. However, in this case, I think we can safely say there *are* two types of people in the world: those who understand why it'd be cool to have a donkey in your backyard and those who don't.

Nonetheless, I settled on ducks. I'll concede that not everyone would want to keep ducks, but I'm pretty sure everyone understands a man who enjoys a duck's company. Who doesn't like ducks? Even the people who inhabit the fanciest of neighborhoods want a lazy walking path that runs by a shallow water element, so on the weekends they can take the kids to stuff park ducks with stale bread.

When a coworker mentioned that her ducks had taken to keeping secret nests and hiding their eggs and that she was knee-deep in ducklings, I offered to adopt two. I did not take into consideration that ducks complain about everything. They quack when I've overslept and left them too long in an enclosure; they quack when our dogs get too close; they quack when they've run out of food; they quack when neighborhood cats stroll into the yard. I didn't realize this until it was too late, but it didn't matter. They were yellowish and soft, one slightly larger than the other, and we named them Yogi and Boo-Boo, and I was smitten.

For a few days, the ducklings lived corralled in a corner of my home office with a large plastic bowl suitable (I thought) for drinking and bathing. These ducks, however, were a bit high-strung, and each time I entered their space, they made a mad dash to hide behind the piano. If I tried to pick one up, they waddled through their food, tripping ass over teakettle, splashing and spilling their water, quacking *murder, murder, murder.*

When I was young, I collected dead butterflies, placed them in empty cough drop tins, and buried them. In my memory, the butterflies are small and solid yellow. However, the closest match I've found on websites dedicated to Kentucky insects is a yellow butterfly called a Cabbage White, which have a white swatch along both wings, tipped with a black dot. So, apparently, I've misremembered. This detail, however, is clear: I was fascinated with the mystery and ritual of church services and so would recite snippets of the twenty-third Psalm (*Yea, though I walk through the valley of the shadow of death*) while decorating the fresh graves with dandelions and white clover.

Most children, I imagine, have a quiet obsession with death shortly after they first begin to grasp the concept. My understanding started the evening my mother was reading to me from a large, white, illustrated Bible. The story was about the prophet Elijah being swept away to heaven in a chariot of fire. The exact question I asked my mother is lost to me, but it was something like: "how does God decide who dies and who doesn't?" I also don't recall my mother's exact response, only that I've been devastated by the answer ever since.

Burying dead butterflies seems a grim pastime for a child but portends the hopeless attraction I would develop toward Romantic poets.

Think of lines from Percy Bysshe Shelley's *Adonais*, the elegy he wrote after John Keats died at twenty-five of tuberculosis:
He is a portion of the loveliness
Which once he made more lovely.

On the other hand, ushering deceased insects to the afterlife might have less to do with being maudlin and more to do with being isolated. We lived in the woods with few neighbors, and my closest friend was my older sister. One of my mother's favorite stories is about how, until my sister started kindergarten, I never spoke because my sister always spoke for me.

These days, my sister and I talk to one another so infrequently that when she does call, I always assume it's to tell me that someone has died. I should call her more often. It's not as though we've had a falling out or are separated by different time zones (we've never lived farther than three hours apart). It's simply the busyness of life: spouses and children, careers, different interests and political views. A gradual growing apart.

And so, late one evening, two years ago, when her name appeared on my phone, I answered with a vague sense of dread, which turned out to be the correct premonition but for an incorrect reason. Her husband had been diagnosed with Amyotrophic Lateral Sclerosis, otherwise known as ALS or (when we were growing up), Lou Gehrig's disease.

"Oh shit," I said.

"Oh shit," she agreed.

In grade school, I was taught that profanity is an indication of a limited vocabulary. The past few years, however, I've read a slew of articles (written, presumably by very smart people) arguing that science suggests there's a link between frequent use of profanity and higher intelligence. Since I curse excessively and carelessly, I accept these findings without question. *Oh shit* in response to my sister's news, however, was not a demonstration of my inflated sense of intelligence, but rather the first and only thing that came to mind. Perhaps if I didn't know anything about ALS, I might have regaled my sister with questions regarding the management of promising treatments, doctors' hopes for a cure, best case scenarios. What I knew, however, is there's no cure for the disease, that it typically moves through a person's body swiftly and ruthlessly, that it is the worst kind of death sentence, destroying muscles and movement until the body suffocates itself.

"Oh shit," I said.

"Oh shit," my sister agreed.

One thing you may not know about ducks, especially if your experience is limited to tossing breadcrumbs to white, pristine domesticated ducks or viewing, from a distance, the devastatingly beautiful plumage of a Wood or Mandarin duck, is that they shit. A lot. On walkways and back porch steps, in their food and water. Ducks also need lots of water, to drink, to play and bathe in, to float as they (presumably) contemplate life. *Like a duck to water* isn't simply a clichéd simile; it is a fact of life. If, by chance, you've been trying to decide between adopting a duck or a fish, I'm here to tell you, it makes no difference: a duck may as well be a fish with two webbed feet. You might be thinking I am somewhat dim not to have realized how much water ducks require, that I am unfit to be a keeper of ducks, and you might be right. However, if you have not tried your hand at duck husbandry, then maybe you're not the one to judge.

After they outgrew their Tupperware bowl, I moved them to an enclosed area in the backyard, dug a shallow indention in the pen, set a plastic paint roller tray in place, and filled it with water. The ducks were delighted, swimming around, dunking their heads, drinking. Within a matter of minutes, though, the water was murky with dirt and poop. Next, I bought a five-gallon rubber container, filled it with water, and stacked stray bricks for steps, which the ducks enjoyed even more. They grew at an astonishing rate, so finally, I bought a fifty-gallon oblong watering trough, crafted higher steps using stones and wood. The ducks were suspicious at first, but once they ventured into this new pond, they were so enthusiastic that they kept launching themselves over the side and onto the ground. Undeterred, they'd waddle back up the steps in order to splash a third of the water out of the trough by the time they cleaned themselves and played. This larger tank was also filthy by the end of day. Fifty gallons of water is too much to waste, so every couple of days I watered my garden, trees, and compost heaps. One bucketful of shitty water at a time.

I strive to be mindful of how I use dialogue in my essays, but from time to time, I still make stuff up, either because too much time has passed for me to recall what was said, or because I prefer snippets of improvised banter. I have always been somewhat of an unreliable narrator of my own life. However, when it comes to the conversation in which my sister shared the devastating news about her husband, I can say with complete confidence, my initial response was "oh shit." I am fairly certain she agreed in kind.

It might be obvious to some readers, by this point, that I really don't want to write this essay, that I'm not certain how much or what to share, that the parts related to my brother-in-law aren't my story to tell. I could share with you scenes of grieving, full of deep sadness, uncertainty, and anger, but most of them are not my scenes to share. I am also struggling because even though I have known my brother-in-law for over thirty years, I don't feel like I know him at all.

Here's a snippet of a scene I remember:

Many years ago, I gave my brother-in-law a book for Christmas because, well, a good book is one of the greatest gifts one can give (and receive). One of my favorite writers, Larry Brown, had published a collection of essays called *On Fire*, and since my brother-in-law was a fireman, I thought this would really be an opportunity for us to connect.

"Don't buy Chip books," my sister told me a few weeks later.

"Oh," I said. "Hit too close to home?" I asked. Not everyone likes to spend their leisure time reading about what they do for a living.

"He really doesn't read books," she said.

Doesn't read books? I thought. *How could you marry someone who doesn't read books?* I wondered if my sister was trapped in a loveless marriage. *Blink twice if you're in trouble.*

Many years later, I was sitting in their kitchen and noticed a book titled something like *The Comprehensive Guide to Humane Butchering of Beef Cattle*. My sister and brother-in-law, along with my parents, had recently purchased ten acres together, and my brother-in-law had bought a few head of cattle.

"Are you really going to slaughter your own cows?" I asked, nodding toward the book.

"Yep. I think so," Chip said. He is six-four, has a black, bushy moustache, and (at the time) pulled people out of burning buildings for a living. He carried himself with a confidence I could never quite muster. Of *course*, he was going to kill cows with his bare hands.

The next time I visited them, my sister was telling a story about Chip's first trip to the slaughterhouse. He cut in.

"Everybody had grown so close to the cows," he said, "so I asked the guy at the slaughterhouse if it was possible to, you know, trade beef with someone else."

"That's reasonable," I said.

"The guy looked at me with a blank stare," Chip said. "So, I tried again: 'you process my cow and then give me someone else's cow to eat?'"

"The slaughterhouse for sissies is down the road," my sister said, imitating a gruff voice.

"No," Chip said. "He didn't say anything. He just shook his head. Looked disgusted."

"I thought you were going to do it yourself," I said.

THE RISK INVOLVED

"Oh that," Chip said. "I made it halfway through the third chapter and decided there was no way I was slaughtering a cow."

It was then I realized maybe my brother-in-law and I had more in common than I suspected. I can't count the number of times my worldview has drastically shifted due to the influence of a book.

When I read Eric Schlosser's *Fast Food Nation: The Dark Side of the All-American Meal*, I stopped eating fast food for almost a year. This decision was less motivated by the reminder of how hazardous burgers, fries, and sugary drinks are to your health, and more to do with Schlosser's recounting of the horrors of factory farms and slaughterhouses, both for the animals and the people who work in them—all for our gastronomic pleasure. I don't recall when I started eating fast food again (and I still do, on occasion). When I pulled the book off the shelf a few days ago to check the publication date, I saw it was published in January 2001. Perhaps as the days wore on after 9/11, I figured there were more hopeless things in the world than worrying about my health, the safety of migrant workers in slaughterhouses, and the ethical treatment of animals. I could be wrong. How to hold multiple horrors (immediate and existential) in your mind? Simultaneously.

A few months ago, some creature of the night tore open one of the chickens and left it to die. The chicken, however, lived severely wounded throughout the day. I typically leave work before sunrise and was at the office (an hour away) with a full slate of meetings before me when my wife called with the grim news. She had tried to employ the help of several neighbors, but they politely declined (and, for the record, I don't blame them). When I arrived home, late afternoon, and assessed the damage,

I realized this chicken was not going to recover. I thought about how disgusted I've always been with the idea of treating animals as though they aren't sentient creatures. So, how to justify spending thousands of dollars on an ill or injured cat or dog (as we've done numerous times) and deciding not to contact a veterinarian with questions about an injured chicken? There is a disconnect, a hypocrisy, in what I'm going to share next, and you may judge me for it (and, for the record, I don't blame you).

I caught the chicken as quickly as I could, wrapped an old t-shirt around her head, and wrung her neck.

Shortly after I started keeping bees, I found one writhing on our back door steps. It appeared to be injured, unable to fly, but still full of furious life. I studied it a few moments, trying to ascertain how best to assist an ailing insect. The only thing that disturbs me more than the possibility of death is watching a creature suffer. And so, despite my misgivings, I gently ground the bee beneath my shoe.

Days later, I shared the incident with Carlton, my friend who sparked my interest in keeping honeybees.

"The bee was still alive," I told him, "but clearly suffering."

Carlton paused and raised an eyebrow as he did when skeptical (which was often).

"So," he said, "what did you do?"

"I didn't think I could help," I said. "So, I ended its suffering."

Carlton did not respond.

"That was the right thing to do, right?" I asked.

"That is always the question, isn't it?"

He offered no more opinion on the matter. The killing of the solitary bee occurred before my many misadventures with bees, such as the time our dog ran through the house, his thick fur full of bees; an afternoon that ended with my wife and I using tennis shoes to squash bees against the bedroom windows. Before the day I harvested honey and then burned my hives because we'd sold our land and were moving to the suburbs. And long before I started helping folks out by removing swarms from church walls and sheds, saving what bees and honey I could before sucking up the stragglers with a shop vac. However, whether I'm making decisions on whether I can save bees or need to destroy them, extend a beloved pet's life by spending thousands at the vet, even the best way to eradicate six baby possums from our washing machine (in case you're wondering: I trapped them one-by-one and released them near a creek a half-mile from our house)—every single time, I think of some version of my question to Carlton: "ending suffering is the right thing do, correct?" The answer is buried somewhere in his silence.

My brother-in-law has lost his power of speech.

We've seen him only half a dozen times since his diagnosis two years ago, and the transformation each time is shocking. At first, I noticed his hand tremor as he passed a pan of mashed potatoes across the dinner table. Six months later, he moved around the house on a motorized scooter. Within a year, he had a tracheotomy and a feeding tube and rarely left his home hospital bed. He speaks with a barely audible whisper, which requires those of us who do not spend hours at his side to attempt reading lips. My sister has become his translator, filling in gaps, anticipating where a thought is headed, and completing most of his sentences.

The many times my wife or I have asked "what can we do," the answer is always "nothing." There's nothing you can do. A few months ago, however, at Thanksgiving, my sister asked if I'd watch the afternoon football game with my brother-in-law in the bedroom; it was for her husband's sake, but I doubt she understood what a great kindness it was to ask me to do *something*. Even if that something was sitting, mainly in silence, watching grown men bash into one another on television. It was *something* the men in our family have done together on Thanksgiving Day for decades. It almost felt normal. When a player made a spectacular play, I'd turn to my brother-in-law and say "that was impressive" or "what a hit," and he would nod his head, mouth a "wow" that I could understand. I was in a recliner wedged between the ends of the hospital bed and their king-sized bed, so I had to crane my neck around to see him. Sometime during the second quarter of the game, I turned to find him sleeping. Or at least, I assumed he was sleeping; he may have grown weary of trying to pretend we were just two guys hanging out, of trying to pretend that all he had to say was "wow," of trying to pretend he wasn't losing his mind because his body has failed him. I watched the game until halftime and quietly went to join the noisy conversation in the living room.

The day after I wrung my wounded chicken's neck was a Saturday, and my wife woke me early, a sure sign that something else terrible had occurred. Whatever mauled the chicken had returned in the night and torn up one of the ducks.

One of the writer's greatest magic tricks is to use words to recreate an image in such vivid detail that readers can see it their heads. I can't bring myself to do that with this duck.

Suffice it to say, he was still alive, and I couldn't figure out how that was even possible. Hence, the aforementioned trip to Wal-Mart for the ax. Within twenty-four hours of killing my first chicken, I was chopping off the head of one of my beloved ducks.

I experienced a near paralysis that almost prevented me from killing the duck; however, what stuck with me for the remainder of the day, in the following weeks, even now as I recount this, is my culpability.

THE RISK INVOLVED

Even though I spent most of the first weekend we had ducks, building them their own outdoor shelter, they refused to enter the space on their own, which if you saw it, would baffle you. One wall is comprised of an antique, wooden sash window, which allows for plenty of sunlight in the morning. The remaining walls are made of old fence pickets and door trim, meticulously cut and pieced together to give the house a classic beadboard look. The tin roof is slanted for rainwater to run into their pond. A thick layer of wall-to-wall, shaved wood chips blanket the floor. There's a duck-sized door on one end (from an old bathroom cabinet) that can be latched from the outside for peace of mind. And finally, the house is perched on solid foot-high piers to discourage things that crawl at night. The word you would use to describe it is *charming*.

The ducks hated it.

Each night at dusk, while the chickens dutifully retired to their coop, we had to chase the ducks around the pen, shooing them into their house while they quacked *murder, murder, murder.*

Once the ducks were full grown, I decided to stop terrifying them each night by stuffing them into their charming house and allowed them to sleep where they chose. Most nights they slept on the ground, side-by-side, near their house. Sometimes, they floated on water all night. And, after months passed with no actual murders occurring in our backyard, I also no longer dragged myself out of my recliner after dark every night to close the door to the chicken coop. This complacency, however, led to what I'd once feared would happen—a fox or owl, possum, raccoon, massive housecat (everyone has their theories) snuck into our yard and severely wounded two of my birds. A false sense of security that leads to the mauling of one chicken is, perhaps, excusable. Not thinking a predator would attack two nights in a row is inexcusable. The only thing worse than watching a creature suffer is the knowledge that you caused it or, at the very least, could have prevented it.

Spring break of my freshman year of college, I went on a youth group trip, and when my mother picked me up from the church parking lot, she was wearing sunglasses. I realized I'd never seen her wear them unless she was driving. She asked about the week as we drove home and then finally said, "your sister has cancer." I don't recall the details of the remainder of the drive, but I'm sure she explained it was Hodgkin's Disease, one of the most treatable forms of cancer, how the doctors caught it early, and that my sister would have surgery to remove the cancerous growth near her collarbone. I do recall that my sister was waiting in the driveway when we got home. She was smiling. I was smiling. Then I hugged her and wept uncontrollably.

"Don't be stupid," she said. "I'm probably not going to die."

She was twenty-two at the time and had recently moved back home to save money for her upcoming wedding. I remember lying on the floor of her bedroom in the following weeks, talking about our fears, religion, and the afterlife. She didn't die, but chemotherapy and radiation were nasty and exhausting. Her hair grew back in time for the wedding the following year. She became a music teacher, gave birth to a son and a daughter, and these are the missing years, the years we saw one another at holidays and once or twice during the summer, the years during which I also got married, started and switched careers, earned degrees, ushered daughters and a son of my own into the world. The years we grew apart.

And then, a few months after my sister turned forty-seven, my mother called to tell me my sister had suffered a massive heart attack; she was alive, in the hospital, but not in great shape. The doctor called it "the widow-maker." In the ensuing months, she had a defibrillator and a pacemaker installed. Put her name on the heart transplant list. But the night she had the heart attack, had my brother-in-law not been at home, was not a first-responder himself, had not known exactly what was happening and exactly what he should do, then my sister probably would have died.

THE RISK INVOLVED

This was all before my brother-in-law's ALS diagnosis, and every day I pray that my sister's heart (in every sense of the word) would continue to heal. To stop breaking.

And this: back when we were both in our early twenties, back when she was recently engaged and received the horrible news that she had cancer, I had never been in a serious romantic relationship, and I thought the most uncharitable thought possible about my future brother-in-law: *I bet he doesn't stick around for this.* I couldn't fathom marrying someone who might crush your heart by dying young. I was, of course, dead wrong. After thirty years, I may not know my brother-in-law well, but I do know this: he accepted the *in sickness and in health* part of the wedding vows a year before he and my sister said them aloud at the altar in front of God and everybody. For that, I love him dearly.

"I think I finally figured you out," my sister told me several years ago. It was one of those rare occasions that she called just to talk. She was still teaching at the time and was just leaving a professional development workshop.

"Oh God," I said. "What?"

"You have a growth mindset, and I have a fixed mindset," she said.

"Oh yeah," I said. "I've read something like that."

"I just need to know what the answer is, how to do it, and I'm good."

"And me?" I asked.

"You always think you have to learn more than anybody else about everything."

"That sounds about right," I said.

"You never stop," she said.

"I know," I said.

There are two types of people in the world: those who appreciate the clarity of black and white, and those who muddle through, lost in the shades of gray.

JEFFREY UTZINGER

Scenes, when they drift back into our memories, often remind us we've misremembered the way we think things are. When I was in high school, my brother-in-law taught me to play Chess and Risk and a version of Monopoly in which you take no prisoners and play for hours. One Christmas break, he and I rolled dice, exchanged money, moved pawns and plastic armies for so long, for so many days, that my mother banned board games for all future holidays.

And this: in college, I house sat for my sister and brother-in-law for a few weeks, and I found my brother-in-law's five-cassette box set of *Bruce Springsteen Live 1975-1985*. I drove around for the remainder of the summer, listening to Springsteen tell stories, wail on a harmonica, and sing songs that made me imagine he understood absolutely everything about my life. I have no memory of talking to my brother-in-law about Springsteen, of asking him if I could borrow the box set for the next few years (and, in fact, never return it), of telling him he unwittingly introduced me to a soundtrack that still runs through my head like well-worn tales passed down through a family.

And this: one weekend he and I decided to drive out to my wife's grandmother's farm to fish, but first we took a detour to a little town neither of us had been to in order to visit a legendary Texas meat market. The heat and smoke from an open pit hit us as soon as we stepped inside, and a guy who looked as old as the town itself asked if we wanted beef, chicken, or pork. Cash only. As we were getting back in the truck, we paused to admire the hundred-year-old county courthouse, visible above the roofline of the meat market. It's a stunning building with spires, mansard roofs, and a massive town clock.

"It'd be great to live in a little town like this someday," I said.

"Yep," Chip agreed. "It would."

These were the days before GPS and cell phones, and since I have a terrible sense of direction, I got us hopelessly lost after we left the meat market. Eventually, we found the right road and made it to the farm in time to spend a few hours pulling catfish and largemouth bass out of a stock tank until dusk.

The night after I chopped off one of the duck's heads, we chased the lone survivor into the coop with the chickens. She cried *murder* before, during, and after we'd closed the door. She was unhappy for several evenings until finally, she started acting like one of the flock. Our chickens do indeed have a pecking order—each morning they are lined up in the same spots along the shelf, waiting their turn to fly the coop. I was delighted one morning to find the duck in line with the others. She lays her eggs in the same nest with the chickens, and they all, more or less, stick together throughout the day, foraging throughout the backyard and napping beneath their favorite holly bush.

I got the duck a plastic, child-size swimming pool that is easy to get in and out of and doesn't require fifty gallons of water. Occasionally, she will still be in her pool after dusk, long after the chickens have retired to the coop. Once she sees me, she waddles out of the water to scurry inside, so I can shut the door behind her. In those few minutes before this, however, I'll watch as she floats alone on the water, and I wonder what she's thinking, if she's thinking at all. I like to imagine she's remembering her friend on those nights, but good God, she saw me wielding the ax. It's better to think she's wishing the water was deeper, that the world was full of more crickets and small frogs.

Just another thing I'll never know for sure.

The opening of Larry Brown's *On Fire* is a two-page essay, a meditation really, that reads like a prose poem in which he uses the phrase *I love* at least fifteen times to describe his passion for nearly everything related to being a firefighter: rappelling the side of a building, using the Jaws of Life to tear open a car, the feel of his gloves and boots, the sirens, the smoke, the adrenaline, and the camaraderie—more than anything else—the camaraderie, with other firefighters at his station.

I assume all the things Brown extols would resonate with my brother-in-law, but I don't know for certain because I never once asked him about his job. For the record: he never asked me about mine either.

I do know this: a buddy who became a firefighter with my brother-in-law, the same year they graduated from college, drives an hour one way, once a week, every week, to give my sister a break from what has become a full-time caretaker's job. He sits at my brother-in-law's bedside for the entire day. And maybe this is it, the essence of living and dying. This, more than anything else.

My sister once told me she knew her husband had a bad shift at the station when he wouldn't share the details. Not only are there things you can see that you can't unsee, there are things you can hear that you can't unhear.

I always assumed when you called 911, your call was strategically routed—if you were being robbed, the police showed up; if injured in a car wreck, an ambulance appeared; if the house is on fire, they send the ladder trucks. Apparently, more times than not, firefighters are the first on the scene, regardless of the situation. So, it's not just that my brother-in-law spent most of his career risking life and limb, rushing in to extinguish fires on precarious structures. He was the first to encounter the broken, the twisted and burnt, the gun shot, the inhuman, unthinkable, seemingly impossible mess of tragedies. The things that call into question truth, beauty, and goodness. The very existence of God.

I can't come to terms with a disease that destroys muscles, breaks down cells of a human body, especially a body that was kept in peak form, ready to respond in the blink of an eye to help the helpless. That this is the body within a matter of months rendered immobile, reduced to mouthing words and tapping fingers. It's an absurd, unfair, gross joke of life. And, if anyone could push back on the idea that the human existence isn't random, it might be a firefighter. A firefighter might say—*no, this is exactly the world's cruelty.* It's not, however, my place to speak for anyone.

Only myself: I have never wanted to know what firefighters encounter on a daily basis. I rush away from fires, literal and figurative, to assess the situation from afar. Usually in hopes that if I ponder the situation long enough, someone else will arrive, ax in hand, with buckets and buckets full of life-saving water.

WHY DON'T YOU DO IT YOURSELF

Building a greenhouse during late June in Texas is either the height of folly or a testament to the belief that someday, this summer, it will rain. *You know, it seems unlikely we'll dip below freezing tonight*, a friend said as he watched me cart lumber to my backyard. It was a joke, but at 8:30 a.m., we were both already wiping sweat from our brows. In the ensuing days, as the frame took shape, a girl from the neighborhood guessed I was constructing a butterfly sanctuary. The neighbors feared it was a second chicken coop. The city didn't care one way or another; they just wanted a site plan and the twenty-five-dollar permit fee.

We live on .5649 of an acre in a sprawling, eighty-year-old ranch-style house surrounded on three sides by neighborhood streets; the backyard is fenced with waist-high white pickets, which means anyone who lives nearby, is walking by, or even driving by has an opinion on what I am doing, how I am doing it, and occasionally, whether I should be doing anything at all.

The first time I saw this house, I recoiled at the faded yellow vinyl siding, the three streets that pinned in the yard, the rotting wooden fence, the driveway barely the length of a car. The interior was worse. When the home inspector sat down with us to review his report, he said, *well, the doorbell works.* The house has three bathrooms and two of the showers didn't function; all the sinks leaked; the toilets needed constant plunging. The pipes beneath the house were corroded, the wiring out of code, every wall painted seafoam green. The hot water heater was pocked with rust. An electrician told me all the breaker boxes needed to be replaced because *that particular brand of box doesn't actually trip when there's a surge.*

Christa, however, loved the house; the bank approved the loan; the neighbors brought fried chicken the first night. How bad could it be?

Within a year, one of the new breaker boxes caught fire in the middle of the night anyway. The flames, contained within a wall, snuffed out before doing major damage, but it served as a harbinger of our relationship with this house: something breaks or wears out, is replaced or repaired in time for something else to fail, followed by something else, then something else, until we're right back to replacing breaker boxes, toilets, caulk, and coats of paint. For the first few years, I assumed I could fix things well enough to hold on until we could leave broken under skirting and curling linoleum for someone else to deal with while we escaped to another house, farther out from the din of noise, somewhere among trees, near a body of water to fish. What I did not envision was living here for fifteen years, the longest amount of time I have lived in the same town, let alone the same house. Building a greenhouse in my yard, something more permanent than garden boxes, something that I didn't rebuild like a fence, or reconfigure like the old storage shed I turned into the chicken coop, seems to indicate that, after years of making plans to escape, I have decided to stay.

The site chosen for the greenhouse, due to shade and a desire to leave an open space for gatherings, meant that I was building a structure thirty feet from one of the busiest streets in town. San Jacinto provides the only north/south route through town that is unimpeded by stoplights or multiple stop signs. One of the only places drivers are required to stop on the mile-long stretch is a four-way intersection catty-corner to my backyard. Emergency vehicles siren their way through all hours of day and night; it's a main artery for school buses as well as a favorite path of seemingly everyone who has some other place to be. My backyard is a cacophony of squealing tires, frantic brakes, impatient horns, and the jackhammer-like reverberations of diesel engines. And anyone walking by, more often than not, sticks their head over the fence to begin a conversation. People seem to view me working in my yard as a cry for help.

That said, I did spend over $25,000 when I moved to town fifteen years ago to ensure that everyone in town knew my name. Every month, I mailed a postcard with my picture and a message informing recipients that I was open for business, standing by to assist with their insurance and financial services needs. For a year, my visage peered down from a billboard overlooking the Wal-Mart parking lot. I bought advertisements on menus, football schedules, magnets, and calendars.

This is a rural community in Texas, however, and people still want to shake your hand and look you in the eye. A standard greeting for newcomers is *y'all found a church yet?* We did, and we joined, and over the next seven years, I served as the church treasurer and council president, helped with Vacation Bible School, delivered meditations when the pastor was on vacation. I served as president of the Kiwanis Club and on the executive board of the Chamber of Commerce. Volunteered for every community service opportunity and fundraising event: worked gates and parked cars at rodeos, carnivals, and 5K races, served pancakes and chopped beef at festivals on the square, planted flags in people's yards on patriotic holidays, delivered meals to the elderly, sponsored youth sports teams, and made charity bids at the junior livestock auction in hopes that my picture would appear in the local paper, standing next to a farm kid and her prize pig. I enjoyed almost every minute of it. I did it for name recognition, so people would do business with me, so I could pay my mortgage and provide for my wife and three children. I did it because prior to moving to town, I had no idea what a Chamber of Commerce actually did, had never played poker with a District Attorney, been part of an organization that said a prayer and the Pledge of Allegiance before every meeting, or lived anywhere that I knew nearly everyone by name, face, occupation, or gossip. I sacrificed weekends and evenings, ran up large lines of credit exactly so that I would become the type of guy you would interrupt to ask about his children when he was in the backyard cutting grass.

Of course, building a structure comprised almost entirely of glass is just daring people not to stop. The greenhouse I've been building for years in my mind is comprised of discarded wooden sash windows, and on nightly walks, I have passed up the opportunity to collect dozens of discarded windows. The timing, though, for such a project has never been perfect: something more practical—remodeling a kitchen or rebuilding a fence—has always prevented me from gathering windows. That, and our garage doubles as an excess storage space and workshop, so recycled materials for projects with no deadlines don't fit.

One late spring afternoon, however, my wife and I were returning from the feed store with chicken supplies when she pointed out a stack of windows on the curb of a resale shop that had recently closed.

"I bet they're cracked and broken," I said.

We made a U-turn and stopped anyway.

"Looks like they came from a mobile home," Christa said.

"They probably won't fit in the van."

Our van is a boxy little vehicle, the kind usually favored by delivery drivers, but despite our attempts to pass up this gift of free glass, most of the windows were neither broken nor cracked, and twelve pieces—the longest six by two feet; the others approximately three-foot irregular squares—all slid neatly into the back of the van. And suddenly, I had windows around which to build a greenhouse. The only thing I didn't have was a plan.

JEFFREY UTZINGER

The Self-Sufficient Homeowner, one of the many DIY books I have accumulated over the years, has a simple greenhouse design, and despite my reluctance to read directions and take advice from others, I figured it would give me a place to start. I was uncertain how the frame could be adapted to hold panes of glass rather than the heavy plastic the plans called for; however, the nice thing about building a structure is you really can't start with anything other than a foundation. I bought eight-foot landscape timbers and cut a few feet off two of them in order to make my greenhouse a rectangle shape. Once I screwed the ends of the timbers together, I drilled several holes in each plank and secured the base to the ground with two-foot pieces of rebar. Fifty square feet seemed small, but I'd chosen eight-foot timbers because that's as big a piece of wood I can fit in our little van. Once I filled the foundation with pea gravel, I stood in the middle, with arms outstretched, and decided crafting spaces of one's own making, designed primarily for one's own use, are good regardless of size. My reverie was broken, however, when my twelve-year-old son sauntered out to take a look and asked if the greenhouse was going to have a basement.

In a region that averages zero annual inches of snow, where the temperature might dip below freezing a dozen or so days out of the year, and where there's rarely ice or a hard freeze for more than twenty-four hours, there seems little need for greenhouses. The times I have lost vegetation to a heavy frost were due to my own impatience, planting out of season, or plain neglect. Last fall, sweet potato slips took over the ledges of my office windows, so I risked planting them in an outdoor bed where they thrived for a few weeks before succumbing to an early cold front. Every few years, sucked into the illusion that mild nights will never end, I plant tomatoes that get frost bitten, wilt, and die. And there's a trio of hanging plants on our front porch that appear to the untrained eye to be ever-present; however, they are forgotten more winters than not. They freeze, are composted, and replaced. Some years, however, the mild nights do run the course of winter, and I've enjoyed homegrown green beans in November and kept bell pepper and jalapeño plants alive and producing for several years. There really is, then, only one plant we own who benefits from the forecaster's warning of *protecting plants, pets, and pipes*: the mighty Staghorn fern.

A decade ago, our neighbor gifted us a Staghorn fern, a tropical plant roughly the shape of a medicine ball whose foliage, as the name implies, resembles the majestic antlers of a deer. These plants can weigh up to three hundred pounds and ours, at its peak, probably reached a hundred. Every few years, however, the neighbor graciously severs the fern with his machete, leaving one half for us to nurture and subdividing the other half into smaller sections he binds to pieces of wood to start a new family of ferns. In rainy years, our newly halved section seems to regain its girth by about a third. We've never tested the fern's aversion to the cold because each fall when the oppressive summer heat finally relents, my neighbor stops by to say *it's about time to move the fern* which if you haven't seen a fully mature Staghorn fern, it might not strike you with the dread that it strikes me and other neighbors who get recruited for the Fern Moving Hour. The move from my backyard where the fern hangs from a chain looped around a sturdy tree branch, across the street to my neighbor's greenhouse requires a ladder, channel locks, a length of two by fours, leather gloves, extra wire, S Hooks, towels for shoulder padding, a tolerance for profanity, and three full-grown men of reasonable strength. In the process, we literally stop traffic. And, I know that springtime has returned—not by robin sightings—but when my neighbor announces *it's about time to move the fern*, and we repeat the migration in reverse.

In addition to the desire to house one's own gargantuan fern, I also want a greenhouse because I grow impatient for spring. When the days shorten and skies turn gray, my wife senses my restlessness and begins saving tin cans from dinner preparations, carefully washing them, and leaving them to dry by the sink. *I saved a can for you*, she'll say, and I begin scrounging the garage shelves for packets of seeds bought in excess over the years. I punch small nail holes in the bottoms of the cans, fill them with dirt from the garden plots, and plant as though my family's survival depends on it. Sometimes I remember to shorthand mark cans with permanent marker—*broc, greens, tom*, but mostly I just let whatever I might have planted grow into whatever it might become. The problem with my can planter menagerie in the garage is the aforementioned lack of excess space. By late February, the corner of every workbench, laundry table, and ledge is lined with containers surrounded by water stain rings. More than half of the seeds never germinate, but a few make it all the way to the garden plots and eventually return to the kitchen as a broccoli head, lettuce leaf, or tomato. Mainly, though, the flurry of winter seed planting is an exercise performed to slake my insatiable desire to be outside, tinkering with plant life, wood, stones, and dirt.

After the greenhouse foundation was in place, I spent several days studying the *Self-Sufficient* plans, measuring and re-measuring my panes of multi-sized glass and making sketches in a notebook. The detail that presented the largest challenge was how to construct the roof, which is a skill you really don't need in life until the time comes when you need to construct a roof. I studied our chicken coop, the eaves on our house, the decorative wishing well. Even though the roof was the final piece, I needed to determine the style because the roof dictates wall height and door placement. All my existing roofs are gable, which is in line with what the *Self-Sufficient* recommends, and so I settled on an eight-foot pitch that would slope down to five-foot-high walls. After several days of gathering material, assembling and disassembling drawings on pages of paper, and laying a foundation, I finally had a plan.

I shoved aside my worktable, piled my wood scrap heap higher, crushed the horde of bicycles closer to one wall, and laid out the frame for wall number one on the garage floor. Building from the ground up would have made the most sense, but I am unable to comprehend marks smaller than a quarter inch on a tape measure, so it helps to see how all the pieces will fit before I commit screws to wood. That, and I decided the panes of glass would rest on the studs of the frame while I built wood sills around them. Building the walls on the ground, then, would allow gravity to work for, rather than against, me. Midway through the first wall, I realized I was going to need twice as many materials than the "cutting list" the *Self-Sufficient* plans prescribed because panes of glass need more support than heavy plastic. I made multiple trips to the local hardware store for more wood, one more box of screws, and then just one more trip for more lumber and screws, and then one final run until, ultimately, I lost count of materials and money spent. I also laid enough caulk to mark the entire perimeter of the county in which I live.

The first wall took several days to construct and blocked the path to the garage door, which is problematic because the garage also serves as our laundry room, and our dryer isn't vented outdoors, and so working with the door closed in July is like spending your day doing manual labor in a sauna. The first few days, I gingerly stepped in the open spaces of the wall frame to heft open our metal garage door, not an easy task due to the door's broken extension spring. At some point, however, I got careless and stepped on a window already secured in place and cracked the glass. Sweaty and swearing, I dragged the wall into our slightly sloped driveway to replace the pane and finish the wall. I caught an occasional breeze, but working in the driveway put me closer to the sidewalk and the street, so I had to stop occasionally to make way for joggers and dog walkers and to talk to neighbors who slowed their cars and rolled down windows to ask if I was ever going to finish this project.

The morning I finally completed wall one, I took a break before attempting to raise it. Standing in the kitchen, drinking coffee, gazing into the backyard, envisioning towering, leafy greens behind walls of glass, my wife asked, "what are you thinking for the roof?"

"A simple gable," I said.

"That's interesting," she said.

Damn it. We have been together for over thirty years and our decision-making process has evolved into an intricate dance of a few spoken words interwoven with an entire backlog of the unspoken. When one of us suggests a place to eat, an idea for a project or a trip, and the other says *I was thinking the same thing*, then the agreement is complete, the plans are made, and we proceed. *That's interesting*, however, spoken by either of us unequivocally means *that is absolutely not at all what I had in mind*. Our friends, who are wiser and older, told us years ago that they negotiate these moments with *I think we have different visions for this. Why don't you tell me yours?* My wife and I's moments of disagreement, however, have not reached that level of refinement.

"Well, tell me what you want," I said.

"Do whatever you like," she said.

This impasse stalled the building project for a few hours and then days.

"What do you think of a slanted roof?" I asked after driving around town, peering into people's backyards.

"I was thinking the same thing," she said. And building recommenced.

A slanted roof meant reconfiguring the wall I had already completed. I needed to add about a foot to the height, which I achieved by removing the wall's bottom board and attaching lengths of landscape timbers to the existing studs. Midway through the extension process, a strange thing occurred: I stopped caring exactly how this structure would function. My building and repair projects rarely go exactly according to plan but always end up doing, more or less, what a set of shelves or new ceiling fans are intended to do. When I tore down our picket fence and rebuilt a new one, I understood its purpose was to maintain the charm of our backyard and allow for a near constant breeze to enter unimpeded while keeping dogs and small children contained. When I turned the storage shed into a chicken coop, it was to house creatures who lay eggs we eat. When I tore out walls, ripped up flooring, and destroyed cabinets, it was to provide more space for food preparation and storage and make way for new appliances. I built massive composting bins out of recycled wood to make my own dirt, to fill garden plots, and grow bigger and better vegetables. The greenhouse I was building had no deadline, no immediate need, something that could ultimately be completely devoid of practical use, and this epiphany allowed me to slow down and lose myself in the process of creation.

A hailstorm hit the night I managed to erect the first two greenhouse walls. Christa and I stood by an open screen door and listened as the pellets drummed our roof and metal lawn furniture. The first spring we lived here, three major hailstorms wreaked havoc on the town over the course of several weeks, and I quickly realized that if you sell insurance, pelting hail is one of the worst sounds in the world as it leads to incessant phones calls, piles of paperwork, and mediating negotiations between adjusters, roofers, and clients. Now that I'm out of the insurance business, however, I no long worry about everyone else's house in a hailstorm; I only have to worry about my own. And really, during this most recent storm, I was fretting about two walls, but as the intensity of the hail grew, I started to laugh.

"What's wrong with you?" Christa asked.

"It just seems kind of perfect, doesn't it?" I said. "You build something out of glass, and the first night it hails."

"You'll be sad," she said.

"I'll start over," I said.

"I'll be sad," she said.

When the storm subsided, I hazarded the frozen pebbles and sharp tree debris to creep barefooted in the dark and survey the damage. All the glass, including the yet unused panes leaning on the fence, were unscathed. I felt relief with a tinge of disappointment. I am as fascinated with the process of creation as I am with the process of destruction—in the natural world, in the narratives of human history, and in my own life. What does it say about me that I find building up and tearing down equally satisfying?

With walls weather-tested and the incline of the roof decided, Christa and I had turned the page, gotten over the hump, found an open window when a door was closed—when you've been with someone thirty years, you accumulate troves of metaphors—it wasn't long, however, before contemplating metaphorical doors become a literal problem with literal doors. And, we have an astonishing collection of doors. There are six ways to enter and exit our home: one in the front, four that lead to the backyard, and one to the garage (which, of course, has two vehicle-sized doors of its own). When we moved in, there were an additional nineteen wooden interior doors, one sliding glass door that led to an enclosed back porch, several sliding closet doors, and one pocket door in the kitchen. Over time, I've removed all the interior doors that aren't attached to a bedroom, bathroom, or closet. Eight of the unhinged doors are hollow, constructed with thin wood and, as it turns out, are useful for garage shelving, props for my children's theatrical performances, and blocking holes in our foundation to keep armadillos from having babies beneath our house. I also have a solid wood door with glass panes that I decided was ideal for a greenhouse.

Because the finer points of geometry elude me, it took a very long time with the ideal door and various lengths of lumber spread out on the lawn before me, coupled with sketches and numbers on a notepad, interspersed with me waving an outstretched tape measure at the sky before I finally determined that this damn door would not work. To simplify: a standard thirty-two-inch-wide door installed in a six-foot wide wall would skyrocket the highest peak of my slanted roof to around thirteen feet. A Blue Norther rushing southward or Gulf hurricane winds raging northward would surely topple a structure this lopsided. Not to mention the thirteen-foot peak would mean the sagging electrical wire that crosses the corner of my backyard would rest on the greenhouse roof.

"Why don't you use one of the doors in the garage?" my wife asked.

"This was in the garage," I said, balancing the no-longer-ideal door against a tree.

"One of the closet doors," she said.

Where were you an hour ago?

Our garage has a small storage closet with a door exactly two feet wide, which I don't believe, in the fifteen years we've lived here, has ever been closed. I rushed to the garage, measured, returned to the backyard, rearranged my puzzle pieces of lumber, and determined that a more slender door would be functional and require only a nine-foot, peaked roof.

"I don't think the fern will fit," my neighbor said once the door was hung.

"Of course it will fit," I said.

Later in the day, I told Christa: "the fern won't fit."

"Of course it will fit," she said.

She always believes things will turn out okay, and I always believe the worst is yet to come but plow ahead anyway. Somehow, together, we work.

The door dilemma solved, along with the fact that my method of framing each pane was sound, filled me with an easy confidence that I was building something that could withstand a bit of wind and hail, and also the curiosity of dog walkers, truck drivers, and neighbors. Yet, there was a remaining element of the greenhouse structure that bothered me. The empty spaces between the roofline and the top of the door and adjacent window formed two triangles, a pattern that was repeated above the south-facing windows. There were also two-foot by two-foot square openings beneath each window and the ground. I figured I could cut corrugated metal or wood to cover the spaces, but the structure thus far was primarily glass and thin strips of wood; it was something that you could look *at* but also something you could look *through*. Any more solid surfaces would mar the illusion. On the other hand, for a greenhouse to be a greenhouse, it needs to hold heat. And then, one afternoon, I finished the beer I was drinking and, before heading inside, wedged the empty bottle in an angle above the door.

"What if we filled all the remaining spaces with empty bottles?" I asked Christa, who was standing at the kitchen sink.

"I was thinking the same thing," she said.

And away we go.

This singularity of vision, however, rather than speeding up the completion of the greenhouse, actually sent the project into the outer realms of opting for form over function. I knew cutting each bottle to size, besides being a task I did not know how to perform, would delay the project even further. However, it seemed a shame not to at least search for a relatively inexpensive tool that easily cuts glass. The internet, in the searching and ordering phase, never disappoints, and within twenty-four hours, I was the proud owner of a bottle cutter. The tool is a linoleum block, roughly the size of a shoebox, with five plastic wheels and one metal wheel mounted to the top and a locking device that allows you to adjust the length of cuts. You simply lay the bottle horizontally on the bed of wheels and make a few turns while the metal apparatus scores the glass. The process makes a satisfying crunching sound as miniscule bits of glass are chipped away, and a jagged equator appears around the circumference of the bottle. It takes mere seconds, but your bottle-cutting journey has really only just begun.

My disdain for reading instructions usually causes only minimal setbacks, but after making several passes on the initial bottle, I began to wonder how many turns it would take before the bottle magically separated.

"You want me to start boiling water?" Christa asked.

"What now?"

"For the hot water bath," she said. "You alternate between boiling and ice water, I think."

What now?

I had, of course, ignored the one page of directions that came with my new contraption. Christa, however, had watched several online videos of consumers using the product.

The process, now that I have successfully separated over two hundred bottles, works something like this: I collect beer and Scotch bottles from my own consumption, wine bottles from my neighbors, and empty condiment or spice jars my wife saves, and let them soak in a metal tub throughout the week. Once I have around twenty bottles, I scrape away the soggy labels and underlying glue, score them, and tote them to the kitchen. I alternate each bottle between a pot of boiling water and a pitcher of ice water until the bottle separates at the seam. About a third of the time, a bottle cracks in the wrong place or the bottom drops out, and I'm left holding shards large enough to shiv a rival inmate.

Different colors and thickness of glass, even brands of booze, require more or less alternate dunks and severity of temperatures. Early in the process, bottles would occasionally split midair and land back in the water, sending hot or cold geysers across the countertop and stove, or worse: they'd hit the floor, and broken glass would skitter throughout the kitchen. One of the rewards of repetitive tasks, however, is the possibility of perfecting a craft. I haven't had a bottle separate in midair for over a month because I can somehow sense when it's about to break apart, so I ensure it always happens underwater. But filling every empty space in the greenhouse walls is going to require around four hundred bottles. I'm not consuming all the alcohol myself; there are friends and neighbors contributing. Still, if you take the number of alcohol bottles, minus ones broken, subtracted from bottles contributed by members outside my household, minus ones that originally contained mayonnaise or cumin, divided by number of days since the project commenced, and well, the solution is there somewhere, but it's not a math problem I'm willing to solve. It's probably not a math problem at all.

Several years ago, a friend who lives in Philadelphia visited our house for the first time. We meandered around the backyard, drinking, catching up, and I started telling him about how I had deconstructed and recreated the white picket fence. I recounted digging holes and setting new posts in cement, how I tried to salvage and restore as much lumber as possible, and of course, how I handcrafted over two hundred new pickets. I described how I ripped cedar planks with a circular saw, used a hand jigsaw to fashion the pointed tip of each picket, and then drilled semicircles on each side to replicate the gothic style. How I developed a system of spacers and levels so that the three hundred and fiftieth picket is the exact same height as the first.

"Wow," he said. "You must have been in a really dark place."

His response caught me off guard, but in the ensuing weeks, I realized he had seen something I missed during that period of my life. Within a year of completing the fence rebuild, a major portion of my life would crumble. Somewhere between the pickets, I must have unconsciously discerned the cracks running through my business. I had gone all in on the mantras that to make money, you've got to spend money, and that God helps those who help themselves. Bootstrap theology, however, is difficult to maintain when you work on 100% commission in a town where most people can't afford the luxury of variable universal life insurance, long-term care policies, and home equity loans. I was spending more on advertising, rent, and employees' salaries than I brought home to support my wife and three young children. Credit cards, loans, and lines of credit were keeping my business and home afloat. And then, the housing market crashed. Payments on home and auto insurance, the only reliable part of my income, moved from late payments to no payments. For a few months, I spent all day calling clients, trying to rework policies to reduce expenses, working old sales call lists to drum up new business, all while sinking under a boulder of debt I could no longer push uphill. A vice president for the company I represented was fond of saying *the first thing you should do when you're in a hole is to stop digging.* So, I stopped digging. I still went to the office every day, but I shut my door and wrote poetry. My favorite subject to write about was the life of John Brown, the father of twelve children and a failed businessman who was sued into poverty and became a domestic terrorist. Not the typical stuff of which poetry is made.

Sometimes not having a plan works out in the end, skipping along on a wing and a prayer, but I couldn't make sixty thousand dollars' worth of debt disappear no matter how hard I tried to stop digging. I was broke in every sense of the word.

"I think we should file for bankruptcy," I said.

"That's interesting," my wife said. "Not something I want to do."

"You must have been in a really dark place," my friend said.

"I'll write you a prescription for antidepressants," the doctor said.

"It costs us nothing to be just," John Brown said.

I was at a loss for words, so I said:

"I was thinking the same thing."

Early in the summer, as I was headed to a semi-monthly poker game, my mother called to tell me that my closest childhood friend had checked himself into rehab. I haven't spoken to him in years, but our families are close, and he had written my mother a long letter explaining how his father's demanding expectations became his own demanding expectations, how the pressures of his job fed into the pressures of his marriage and looped back again, how he was afraid his children were afraid of him, and how alcohol had fueled it all for years and years, kept it afloat, bearable, made it work until he cracked and nearly drowned alone in the darkness.

"I'm worried about him," my mother said.

"He'll be okay," I said.

"Do you think he'll be okay?" she asked.

"He'll be okay," I said.

When she asked *How do you know he'll be okay?* I realized she was no longer asking about my friend. She was asking about me.

Thousands of years ago, the zealot Paul wrote: *For now we see through a glass, darkly; but then face to face: now I know in part; but then shall I know even as also I am known.* In the evenings, as I stand in my greenhouse, sanding the rough edges off the ends of colored glass and then arranging and rearranging pieces in an attempt to make green, blue, brown, yellow, and clear glass appear to be a random mosaic, all the while drinking, I try to stave off the thought that, once again, I must be in a really dark place. I don't know, and I don't want to be known. A weird thought to think standing in a glass structure next to one of the busiest streets in town.

Five months have passed since I started building my greenhouse, the corrugated tin roof is in place, the slim door hung, an old coffee cart that used to be in my insurance office is on one side of the greenhouse, and kitchen cabinets someone left on the side of the road line the other side. A fifty-gallon metal trough catches rain from the slanted roof that I use to water the dozens of small avocado trees that sprouted from seeds one of my daughters and I planted throughout the spring and summer. Last night, the space became a little smaller because Christa and I, using pulleys and rope, hung the Staghorn fern from the rafters. It fit. After Christa left to see to other things, I stayed a little longer to peel away a few more labels, and decided that, if nothing else, this space mutes the rumblings of passing cars and trucks. I am visible, still, to all who pass by, but now I can maintain the illusion of friendliness with a barrier of glass between me and the world.

ACKNOWLEDGEMENTS

"The Seduction of Place" first appeared in The Raven Chronicles, Spring/Summer 1999, Vol. 8, No. 2 and Lynx Eye, Winter 1999, Vol. 6, No. 1.

Note: The phrase "hive-like conglomerations of cellular living" is from Scene I stage directions in Tennessee Williams' play, The Glass Menagerie. An Introduction to Literature, edited by Sylvan Barnet, William Burto, and William E. Cain, Longman, 2011, p. 856.

"Chemical Reactions" first appeared in The Chattahoochee Review, Winter 1999, Vol. 19, No.2 and was selected by Robert Atwan as one of the "Notable Essays of 1999" in The Best American Essays 2000 series.

"Beginner's Luck"

Note: "It isn't such a bad thing, To live in one world forever" is from James Galvin's poem, "Everyone Knows Whom the Saved Envy." Resurrection Update: Collected Poems 1975-1997, Copper Canyon Press, 1997, pp. 11-12. Used with permission.

"The Risk Involved" first appeared in High Plains Literary Review, Winter/Spring 2001, Vol. 16, No. 1.

THE RISK INVOLVED

"Insatiable" first appeared in Lynx Eye, Spring 2002, Vol. 9, No. 2.

"Swarm Season" first appeared in Southwestern American Literature, Fall 2000, Vol. 26, No. 1.

Note: "Brushed with the hiss of rustling wings" is from Book I of John Milton's Paradise Lost, edited by Alexander S. Twobley, Silver, Burdett and Company, 1897. Hathi Trust Digital Library, https://hdl.handle.net/2027/loc.ark:/13960/t9j39c38f.

"Woods Walking" first appeared in Smoky Blue Literary and Arts Magazine Fall/Winter 2023, Issue 19.

"You're Going to Hell for This" first appeared in The Cream City Review, Fall 2002, Vol. 26, No. 2, and was selected by Robert Atwan as on the "Notable Essays of 2002" in The Best American Essays 2003 series.

"Indefinite Light" first appeared in Tampa Review Winter 2004, 26

"Walk Away Slowly (You Know You'll Be Back)" first appeared in Floyd County Moonshine, Fall 2023, Vol. 15, No. 2.

"White Picket Fences"

Note: The phrase "lilacs last in the dooryard bloom'd" is from Walt Whitman's poem "When Lilacs Last in the Dooryard Bloom'd." Memories of President Lincoln, Thomas B Mosher, 1912. Hathi Trust Digital Library, https://hdl.handle.net/2027/uiuo.ark:/13960/t1qf8rb72.

"Count Your Chickens" first appeared in Carve Magazine, Summer 2023.

Notes: The phrase "For many a time, I have been half in love with easeful Death" is from John Keats' "Ode to a Nightingale." The Golden Treasury of the Best Songs and Lyrical Poems in the English Language, Macmillan and Co., 1881. Hathi Trust Digital Library, https://hdl.handle.net/2027/hvd.32044009709692.

JEFFREY UTZINGER

The phrase, "how often I have longed to gather your children together, as a hen gathers her chicks under her wings, and you were not willing" is from Matthew 23:37-39, New International Version. Bible Gateway. https://www.biblegateway.com/passage/?search=Matthew%2023%3A37-39&version=NIV.

The phrase, "those little birds, rejoicing in wondrous fashion, according to their nature, began to stretch out their necks, to spread their wings, to open their beaks and to gaze on him," from Thomas of Celano's The Treatise on the Miracle of Saint Francis was quoted from Saint Francis and Poverty, Benziger Brothers, 1910, p. 56. Hathi Trust Digital Library, https://hdl.handle.net/2027/coo.31924029419292.

"Duck"

Notes: The phrase, "Yea, though I walk through the valley of the shadow of death" is from Psalm 23: 4, King James Version. Bible Gateway. https://www.biblegateway.com/passage/?search=Psalm%2023&version=KJV.

The lines, "He is a portion of the loveliness/ Which once he made more lovely" are from Percy Bysshe Shelley's poem, Adonais: An Elegy on the Death of John Keats, quoted from Shelly Adonais, edited by William Michael Rossetti, Oxford at the Clarendon Press, 1903, p. 88. Hathi Trust Digital Library, https://hdl.handle.net/2027/cool.ark:/13960/t88g9601p.

"Why Don't You Do It Yourself"

Note: The phrase, "For now we see through a glass, darkly; but then face to face: now I know in part; but then shall I know even as also I am known" is from 1 Corinthains 13:12, King James Version. Bible Gateway. https://www.biblegateway.com/passage/?search=1%20Corinthians%2013%3A12&version=KJV.

ADDITIONAL ACKNOWLEDGEMENTS

Special thanks to my parents and sister for supporting my love of reading and writing—y'all are the best. To Dr. Susan Stayton for being an amazing mentor and friend along with her dear husband, John (may he rest in peace). To Kevin Grauke for thirty years of friendship, writing advice, and a thousand fantastic reading recommendations. Thanks to Tom Grimes for being Tom Grimes. The Lockhart Writing Group, especially those who read so many drafts of these essays: Wayne Walter, Phil McBride, Tam Francis, Jessica Rutland, Todd Blomerth, and Laura Adams. My three children, Emma, Lillianne, and Thomas for your love, laughter, and inspiration. And, of course, my wife, Christa, for allowing me to write the history of our lives together, all from my imperfect (often unreliable) point of view.

And finally, thanks to the folks at April Gloaming Publishing for bringing my own unbridled holler to a larger audience.

ABOUT THE AUTHOR

Jeffrey Utzinger spent the first ten years of his life in the woods of Northern Kentucky before his family moved to the suburbs of Fort Worth, Texas. After graduating from high school, he attended college in Austin where he met his future wife. He earned an MFA in Creative Writing from Texas State University while working maintenance at a chemical plant in South Austin. While he and his wife have rarely lived within the Austin city limits, they've never strayed far from the area as they've moved from town to town, job to job. Jeffrey was a college professor, a corporate trainer, and then spent several ill-fated years selling insurance. Eventually he returned to academia, earned a PhD in American Literature from Texas A&M University, and currently serves as a dean and English professor at Concordia University Texas. His creative and scholarly work has appeared in numerous literary and academic journals. Jeffrey and his wife live in Lockhart, Texas where they raised their three children who are in the process of finding their own place in the world. Jeffrey also keeps chickens, a duck, cats and dogs, and a few thousand bees. This is his first published collection of essays.

Milton Keynes UK
Ingram Content Group UK Ltd.
UKHW040651111124
451038UK00009B/139